Praise for *The Haunted House Diaries*

"Best-selling author William J. Hall thrills and chills us again with a tale of a house that is incredibly haunted with his latest book, *The Haunted House Diaries*. It is a must read for those captivated by haunted spaces and places. Bring your flashlight and your courage...you'll need them both!"
—Jim Harold, president, Jim Harold Media LLC; host, Paranormal Podcast, Jim Harold's Campfire, The Paranormal Report, and TV You Grew Up With; author, *Jim Harold's Campfire: True Ghost Stories* series

"This book is a refreshing advancement in the field of paranormal study! The diary is fascinating with its diverse incidents.... The approach the author has taken to this broad case dispels many old school myths and finally provides some real insight into the paranormal."
—Steve Hudgeons, host of The Texas UFO Radio Show

"*The Haunted House Diaries* is, bar none, one of the most terrifying stories I have come across. A simple word of caution before venturing forth and settling in to read this book: double check that the doors and windows are locked firmly, you have your phone close at hand, AND have a flashlight nearby...just in case your lights suddenly snap off for NO reason. Expect no mercy from the contents of this book!"
—Brent Holland, host of *Night Fright Show*, the number-one show of its genre

"William J. Hall has focused his unique investigative skills on a 50-year experience documented by an actual witness. This powerful first-person story is a riveting read supported by an array of photographs for the reader to review and judge on their own. The stories captured in this exciting book display an array of paranormal activity that intrigue the reader to continue—this is not your typical ghost story or investigation.

This is a wide range of paranormal stories that span five generations and continue today! I could not put this down and had to read on to see what was next!"
—Al Warren, host/producer of "The House of Mystery" radio show and host of "WarrenXchange Paranormal Radio Show" on the Z Talk Radio Network Seattle, and host/producer of "Dark Shadows Radio" on BlogTalk Radio Canada

"Author Bill Hall takes you to a small Connecticut town for an intimate look into the world of the paranormal through the mind of one person's personal journal entries. There are years as well as pages of notes, skilled documented investigations, and numerous eye witness accounts. One thing is for sure…after reading the book, you'll never get me within a mile of this house and you can take that to the Vegas bookies!"
—Tina Marie Caouette, host of "Restricted Airspace," Las Vegas

"This is a fascinating book about a paranormal flap that produces all kinds of unexplained activity. This book is a must have for any serious paranormal researcher and a fascinating read for anyone interested in this subject. William J. Hall gets two thumbs up as Siskel and Ebert used to say!"
—Royce "the Redneck Radioman" Holleman, Talknow Radio *http:// talknowradio.blogspot.com/*

Lynne,
Best wishes,
Bill Hall

THE HAUNTED HOUSE DIARIES

The True Story of a Quiet Connecticut Town
in the Center of a Paranormal Mystery

WILLIAM J. HALL

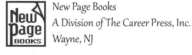
New Page Books
A Division of The Career Press, Inc.
Wayne, NJ

THE HAUNTED HOUSE DIARIES
EDITED AND TYPESET BY GINA SCHENCK
Cover design by Dutton and Sherman design
Printed in the U.S.A.

To order this title, please call toll-free 1-800-CAREER-1 (NJ and Canada: 201-848-0310) to order using VISA or MasterCard, or for further information on books from Career Press.

The Career Press, Inc.
12 Parish Drive
Wayne, NJ 07470
www.careerpress.com
www.newpagebooks.com

Library of Congress Cataloging-in-Publication Data

CIP Data Available Upon Request.

To Paul and Ben Eno

I am sure we are the best of friends throughout the multiverse.

To the Fillie Family

A heartfelt thank you for sharing your journey. You have made a valuable contribution to our ongoing quest to understand the paranormal.

ACKNOWLEDGMENTS

Special thanks to Rita Rosencrantz (my literary agent), Michael Pye (senior acquisitions editor), Gina Schenck (editorial director), Kirsten Dalley (senior developmental editor), Jeff Piasky (cover design), and the rest of the delightful folks at New Page Books. I am humbled by the opportunity to do it all again.

Donna, Bob, Michelle, and Diane: Thank you for your help, enthusiasm, and bravery to share your story, which has spanned so many years.

Paul and Ben Eno for your time, expertise, generosity, dedication to serious paranormal investigation, and, most of all, friendship.

Shane Sirois for your refreshing insight and experience with the paranormal. Your contributions enriched this book and me, and helped make more sense of all of this. I am proud to call you my dear friend.

Marc Dantonio for all of your assistance and expertise with photo analysis, for telling your part of the story, and for being a generous friend.

Ray Swec for the photography, investigation assistance, and of course for the many years of laughter-filled friendship.

Greg Harold for your help in identifying similar entities to Ashwar and sharing your fascinating theories on those entities.

Julie Turner and Nancy Cardone of Jewel Photography for coming to my aid once again for photo prep. Your generosity and support are very much appreciated.

And to *you* reading this. Without you, I am just alone talking to myself on paper.

"Reality is merely an illusion, albeit a very persistent one."

"Time and space are modes by which we think
and not conditions in which we live."

—Albert Einstein

CONTENTS

Part II: Phenomena in the Flap

Part III: Investigation, Theory, and Discussion

Disclaimer

The farmhouse in this book is real. It is a private residence and is not open to the public.

Under no circumstances are the residents to be contacted directly by anyone for any reason related to the house or their story. All direct contact will be refused and ignored.

Any inquiries by anyone for any purpose should be directed to William J. Hall, who owns exclusive rights to the story and acts as a liaison for the family.

NOTE TO THE READER

What you are about to read is a true story. It is based on an investigation that began in 2005 and continues to this day. It features an expanded
and detailed diary of events from notes written over a period of five decades while growing up in the home.

All of the photos and video evidence contained in this book and on
the bonus Website have been examined by a photo and video professional. However, the theories or conclusions presented from evidence
remains the sole opinion of the author unless stated otherwise.

As a result, all reflections, smudges on camera lenses, and other optical effects that are not evidence of the paranormal have been eliminated
from consideration in this work. Note that no photo evidence is fool-
proof. The best that we can present is evidence that appears to have merit
and is considered in our minds to be unexplainable and more likely evidence of paranormal phenomena. This is even more valuable when it is
a component of the overall activity going on.

My experience is that about 98 percent of all "paranormal photos"
are actually misinterpretations of normal camera phenomena unknown
to the casual photographer. This is true even when photographing in areas where there is known phenomena, such as the farmhouse and areas
featured in this book.

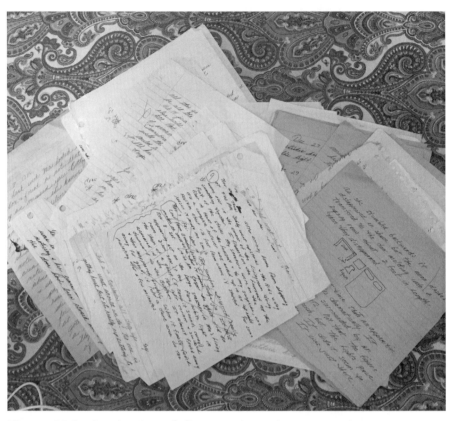

Figure N-1. *A selection of diary entries written on various paper over a period of decades.*

FOREWORD

When I was 16, I began recording accounts of unexplainable experiences in my journal. I have finally transferred it on to a disc and onto a computer. Originally, I had decided to write down everything as it took place and ended up with about 250 pages of experiences. I remember that I began writing things down on the backs of envelopes, in the margins of my kids school papers, and on whatever I had close by whenever something happened. That system lent itself to built-in disorganization, although it did preserve many fascinating observations and occurrences. Fortunately, most of the scraps had been dated. In the end, I had a sizeable box of history that made absolutely no sequential sense. It took me nearly six months of intensive sorting and filing to arrange them in order. When I got my first laptop, I spent many long nights moving the information on to it, piece by piece.

For years I have thought it held the promise of being an interesting first-person account of the phenomena that my family and I have witnessed here. It was meant for future generations that might live in this house. I am proud to see it being expanded upon from the recollections of the family, and written and released so it can be shared on a broader level. Perhaps we can band together and discover additional insights into this mystery that is not only part of my life, but part of all of our lives and very existence.

My family and I would like to thank Bill Hall for bringing my story to the public, and for doing so in an objective manner. We appreciate his keen ability to meticulously research a story and present it to his readers in an open and honest way. I would also like to thank Paul and Ben Eno and Shane Sirois, who have helped so much by being attentive and supportive, and opening our eyes to possibilities we never dreamed of!

—Donna Fillie

Introduction

Paranormal Crossroads

"Mysteries once thought to be supernatural or paranormal happenings—such as astronomical or meteorological events—are incorporated into science once their causes are understood."
—Michael Shermer

The investigation of the house on Lindley Street in Bridgeport, Connecticut (the subject of my book *The World's Most Haunted House*), profoundly changed me. There was no preparation, however, for what lay in my immediate future. The singular, malevolent essence I had encountered in studying the case on Lindley Street would be replaced by a vast variety of fascinating, if often irritating, entities whose existence seemed to intrude not only on one another, but more specifically on the lives in an extended family, which for generations had occupied the farmhouse that sat there at the vortex of a paranormal flap.

There are some areas that are just ripe for paranormal activity. It doesn't mean everyone in that area will experience phenomena. Far from it. Some will go their entire lives without an incident. Others, however, will experience a small piece of phenomena at these virtual paranormal crossroads. They will see a UFO or hear the cry of an unknown animal and then see a new species with their own eyes. Or perhaps a few odd things are happening in their house and have been for years. And some, the few, lie at or near the epicenter of all such activity and experience a mix of all things paranormal.

Litchfield Hills and its surrounding towns contain just such a crossroads. And located in Torrington and Goshen, Connecticut, lies one of the most fascinating and unusual paranormal flaps ever discovered.

Like most wanna-be paranormal investigators, I, too, found myself in the somewhat awkward position of wanting to be a part of it—to witness the unearthly, unexplainable things for myself. My friend and mentor, Paul Eno, explained to me how one has to be psychologically ready for this sort of journey, and it is most definitely not for the unprepared, run-of-the-mill curiosity seeker. One has to adroitly tread the fine lines between that of investigator and intruder, friend and professionally detached skeptic. However, one has to start somewhere and, as is so often the case, it begins with a boundless portion of curiosity. On that count, I certainly fit the bill. I trusted Paul's advice and proceeded with care and caution.

It was during one of our regular luncheon meetings—paranormal investigators Paul and Ben Eno and I—that we began discussing one of the most interesting and varied cases they had ever investigated. This investigation had been ongoing since 2005!

Paul said, "This is more in your neck of the woods, Bill. Right down your alley. Would you like me to introduce you to the family? I'm sure we can arrange for all of us to meet there at the house."

Boy, would I, I thought. It seemed almost too good to be true. Once again, I was filled with the wide-eyed anticipation and heart-pounding joy of a little boy hurrying down that long winding stairway on Christmas morning.

Not long after, it was arranged for Paul, Ben, Marc Dantonio (an astrophysicist), and me to meet at the 1700s farmhouse that sits at the center of the paranormal crossroads in Litchfield Hills, Connecticut. The family was cordial and open, and the relationship built easily and comfortably.

After our initial meeting, as we walked around the knoll and down the hill, Paul turned to me and said, "Perhaps this is book two for you. It certainly is worthy of it."

That paranormal flap is the subject of this work. And one home in particular, located at the epicenter of this activity, is the subject of the haunted diaries contained within and will be our focus for identifying the broad scope of phenomena that transverses this rural area.

Paul was right. And this is it.

—Bill Hall
Plainville, Connecticut
November 2014

Figure I-1. *Aerial still taken from the drone filming of the land for the investigation. Photo still used by permission of Marc Dantonio.*

PART I

THE HAUNTED HOUSE DIARIES

CHAPTER 1

AN INTRODUCTION TO THE DIARY

"Every time we go to the house, there is something new."
—BEN ENO

It was a sunny, November afternoon just after Halloween. I was sitting across the kitchen table from Donna Randall Fillie, the keeper of the diary that is central to this investigation. Her stories—well, really the fascinating snippets from her life—simply enthralled me. They report and document the seemingly unworldly, or perhaps multi-worldly, events that she has witnessed in her life while occupying the historic farmhouse. She thoughtfully reflected on the diary entries as we dug into her experiences with one from the summer of 1972:

I lie awake in the sweltering heat, so not typical for the Connecticut countryside where our old farmhouse stands. How can he sleep [her husband] in this ungodly heat, I think to myself, resentful of his quiet, even breathing.

Up under the eaves in the back bedroom we freeze throughout the long winters, then suffer in pools of sweat through the short, but unpredictable weather of the summers.

Restless, I swing my bare legs over the side of the large antique bed, remembering for a moment that it once belonged to my grandparents. They had a long and happy marriage, raised a family, and lived most of their years in that same house. This bed was a gift to my grandmother at the time they bought their first farm. Those mental ramblings distract me for only a moment and my mind returns to feeling the relentless heat. I slide down onto the floor and make my way around the foot of the bed, ducking, without thinking, under the beam, which supports the slanted ceiling. Maybe the bed in the spare room will offer some comfort or at least dry sheets and more ventilation. In the black quiet I lay down, hiking my flimsy nightgown up to my hips.

Suddenly my eyes flip open. My breathing becomes deliberately short and quiet. There is a hand on the back of my left thigh, seductively rubbing up and down. It is not a physical hand, no feeling of flesh against flesh or the distinguishable massaging of individual fingers, but, nonetheless, a hand-shaped area of pressure. It begins to move, slowly rubbing up and down, back and forth. My skin begins to crawl. Kicking my legs wildly in the frightening discomfort of the moment, I bolt back into my bedroom, waking my sleeping husband. Hysterical as I am, I try to explain what has just occurred.

The events—the encounters—that Donna and Bob have experienced are something more than the typical ghost stories encountered around campfires or, for that matter, even those offered in professional reports or exposés. They do not conform to the more typical single entity encounter. In their lives, a wide variety of paranormal themes have being playing out, repeatedly, across many decades and during generations before them. Five generations of the family have lived in the house currently owned by Donna and Bob.

"And why is it you continue to stay here?" I asked.

Donna shrugged her shoulders. "I honestly don't know! Understand that I am *not* afraid; this is my home. It's all I know. Throughout everything we've seen and heard here in our house, our ties remain strong and unwavering."

The extraordinary old New England farmhouse was built in 1793 and has been home to six generations of the Randall family; Donna and her family have been there for more than 60 of those years. It is extraordinary in size and stark simplicity, in service and security. It is extraordinary in that it was constructed at the point of a paranormal flap

Figure 1-1. *The farmhouse in 1935. The paranormal was a regular occurrence even then. Photo used by permission of Donna Fillie.*

Figure 1-2. *Donna on the family land in 1964. Photo used by permission of Donna Fillie.*

Figure 1-3. *The old barn, which sits on land that still has active paranormal activity. Photo used by permission of Donna Fillie.*

where time and dimensions, life forms and realms, flow together seamlessly; where visitation between and among them occurs more by chance than by plan, more as unexpected bumps in the night than the meeting of well-defined visions.

It is less a haunted house than a path side inn where entities from across time and space and multiple dimensions converge and lodge on their ways toward their individually unique destinations. Donna's family had the nearly exclusive opportunity to engage these essences, witness their endless forms, and become familiar with their obsessions and patterns, their persistence, and, often, their capricious nature.

Within these pages I will share with you their experiences down through the generations, what we believe we have learned, and their own reactions to "them," which range from delight to irritation to exasperation, but rarely fear. Some they recognize; most they do not. But each of them has presented a wonder-filled possibility for the family to gain a glimpse into the elusive and confounding realm of paranormal phenomena.

This house is Donna's home, and like most homes, it has typically been a comfortable, safe, and serene oasis away from the trials and tribulations of the world outside. Unlike most homes, they have always had co-inhabitants who, it appears, also claim the house as their home. Donna grew up learning to be pleased and proud to share.

Donna is not inclined to argue or debate the point. She knows what she has experienced and is content that knowledge is sufficient beyond any arguments others have proposed. There are visitors. She has seen them, been touched by them, been sung to by them. She has seen unsupported orbs in the house with the naked eye, objects move with nothing propelling them, and time slips, and photographed them and recorded the noises and voices of invisible entities. As she explained, they can be very persistent and, in her very human way, she has often had to explain to "them" that it is time for them to shut up and let the family get some sleep.

Few people outside of the family are aware of the situation here, but the ones who have ventured closely into their lives have been changed forever by their experiences.

To the casual observer passing by on his way through the lush green meadows of rural Connecticut, the large, old house is one of the finest examples of authentic Americana that New England has to offer. Listed in the National Archives, it adheres to the stark lack of detail, which is the hallmark of most structures built in 1793. First serving as a general store, it was added on to in the 1880s. It still sits proudly on a low knoll, protected by the mountains at the rear and overlooking the fields and meadows in the valley below.

When Donna was born in 1950, she was brought to this very house straight from the hospital. Waiting for her were a host of family members, all of whom lived in the house at the time. With 13 rooms and an apartment in the basement, there was room to house a large number of people. At that time they included her parents, her sister, Diane, her great grandparents, grandparents, and her aunt Nonie. Life was wonderful at the house with large, beautifully decorated Christmas trees during the winter holidays, picnics and lawn parties filled with laughter during the summers, and regularly demonstrated feelings of love regardless of the season. Among all of that there lurked the constant presence of more than a few unwanted otherworldly prowlers that all too often disrupted their lives.

As a child, it was common for Donna to see and hear a wide array of nighttime apparitions. Hallways echoed with the sounds of footsteps, and the voices of uncountable spirits could be heard engaged in unintelligible chatter or quietly chanting or singing hymns that droned on into the night.

As children, Diane and Donna rarely had the luxury of a full night's sleep because they would be awakened by their parents, if not by the these puzzling visitors, making sure they were still safe in their room. When their parents would hear the hushed voices of the invisible presences, it would initiate the familiar ritual of checking the house and making sure the children were safe in their beds.

Donna's aunt married in 1958 and moved out of the house. In 1962, her grandfather died, followed by her grandmother in 1966. Subsequent to that time, her sister, Diane, also lived in the house. At that time the disruptions by the nightly visitors markedly increased.

When invited to spend the night with childhood friends, Donna was surprised to find an absence of voices and footsteps and the droning melodies that had become such a constant and "normal"—if often irritating— part of her life experience. Their houses appeared to be "clear," as she came to characterize them. She never discussed that aspect of life with her friends, partly because they didn't bring it up and partly because she looked upon it as a relatively normal aspect of life. It was not until much later that Donna would come to realize how unique all of that was to her specific circumstances.

A Personal Note From Donna

This diary follows the hauntings that have been present in my family house throughout my life, but specifically during the period from my late teenage years until 2003. I began this record as a means for personal amusement. Still, I strived to record each situation with as much accuracy as possible. During this period I got married and gave birth to two children. My daughter Michelle was the focus of special attention by these visitors during her childhood. It was more of a trying experience for her than I realized until one day she confided: "I really like to sleep at Charlene's house, Mommy, because it's clear."

Although my family has been deeply affected by the situation in this house, it hasn't been the source of severe mental trauma or psychological problems. What it has done, is to provide us the unique opportunity to peek into another dimension that few have experienced. We have acquired an understanding, of sorts, about what the future holds for us. Upon reflection, we understand that what we have witnessed would send the most stouthearted "outsider" running for their lives, screaming into the cold, dark night. Perhaps we were chosen to witness these events because of our basic level headed nature, our understanding of the world, or because we had no preconceived ideas about what a haunting should be. Whatever the reason, we shy away from the word "haunting," and choose to believe that whatever is here, would, more than likely, rather be somewhere else. There is no panic. There is no ongoing terror. Typically, there is not even any anger—irritation, perhaps, but not anger. We witness no head twisting red-eyed monsters hiding under our beds (at least not yet!). We are content in the knowledge and understanding that we are not alone here in this unique place and time.

~

Author's note: At various places throughout the diary, the reader will encounter passages that are set off in brackets [   ]. These represent commentary and are not part of the diary entry.

Chapter 2

Diary Entries From the 1960s

"I'll just keep writing about it in the hope that I can get a better handle on things if I can keep track of what is actually happening."
—Donna Randall Fillie

Entry #1 (Winter 1966)

Mom and Dad are away, visiting Eunice and Harry tonight. I was watching a movie and enjoying being alone for a few hours. While sitting on the couch, I felt the room grow really cold. Not just a regular type of cold, but a bone chilling, piercing, hug yourself, kind of cold. The heat was on and the furnace was running, but, God, it was so cold! It felt like something was drawing the blood out of my body. It was like dead cold—like every bit of heat in my body was being sucked out of me. When I held my hand a few inches away from my cheek, I could feel the cold radiating from my body. It was all quite bizarre. At one point, the doorknob to the downstairs bedroom started jiggling. Presently, the whole door began shaking. Man, I got scared! I walked up to the door, but I didn't have the guts to open it. Brandy, our dog—usually inquisitive, if not downright nosey—didn't even come into the room to check it out, so I went to get her. Her presence was a source of comfort and reassurance. I had to drag her across the wooden floor. She actually made marks with her toenails as she resisted being moved toward the door. Her hair stood straight up on her back, and she fought hard to get away from me. It was very clear that she did not want to go near that room. As I released her collar, an ice-cold breeze blew by me, strong enough to move my hair and ripple my clothes. Mom and Dad arrived home soon after that. I related the story, still feeling the chill. Dad checked the room. Everything was quiet and nothing had been disturbed. I guess I don't really want to spend that sort of *quiet evening* alone anymore! A lot of weird stuff has always gone on here, but it was never anything we could see. All I know is that now things have begun moving that aren't supposed to. We've had hairbrushes slide across counters and hang in midair. Not long ago a candlestick slid across the stereo and also hung in midair. On one occasion a wreath came off the wall and instead of falling directly to the floor, it landed way out in the middle of the room—something we couldn't duplicate when we tried to replicate the motion.

Entry #2 (Summer 1967)

Dad was lying on his bed upstairs listening to a baseball game on the radio. The floor all around his bed started to "snap" loudly. It was a sharp sound, like the crack of a bull whip. Then the mattress lifted up just a bit—as if someone was under his bed that was too large for the space. He hurried off the bed and looked underneath, but of course nothing was there. It was funny in a way, because he was so disgruntled by it all.

Dad worried constantly about money. He worried about the financial result of people finding out about the things going on in the house. He had a great sense of humor so he didn't take most of the things too seriously—certainly not as threatening. I often compared notes with my mother about the things we witnessed in the house. We would ask each other, "Did you hear that? Did you see such and such?" We sat and philosophized, "What could it be?" Our lives were filled with so many strange things.

Entry #3 (Summer 1967)

So many odd things happen around this house. It is often amusing. Last night the upstairs toilet kept flushing itself. Over and over it flushed. Dad kept getting up to check, but he could find nothing wrong with the mechanism. Everything seemed perfectly fine. I guess just let "them" have their fun, whoever—whatever—they are.

Entry #4 (Summer 1967)

This is really a puzzle. I was sitting on the couch talking with Mom. I was wearing my silver chain as usual. I often put my finger under it and slide my finger back and forth. It's one of those unconscious habits that I'm often not even aware of. After a few minutes, I went to put my finger back to my chain and the chain was gone. I felt down the front of my sweater, then got up and checked the couch cushions and the floor. It was nowhere to be found.

After searching the area, I walked across the room and started up the stairs. On the fourth step, I saw my chain just lying there! It was clasped and the front of the chain was dangling over the front edge of the step, gently swaying back and forth. That chain definitely would not fit over my head without being unclasped. I had not felt a thing as it had been re-moved—*unclasped* and removed! Great, now they're pilfering jewelry!!

Entry #5 (Fall 1967)

Diane washed her hair in the kitchen sink this morning. She set her jade ring on the windowsill and when she reached for it, it was gone. She got really upset and had Dad check the pipes to make sure it didn't go down the drain. She just came downstairs and told us that she found the ring in her jewelry box and all of the other jewelry had been pushed aside to make room for it in the center. Her ring was pressed down into the velvet so hard it left a clear impression. It gave me the creeps because Mom had a similar experience a while back. Mom and Dad had gone away with their friends for the weekend. When they returned, Mom dis-covered that she had lost a ring that meant a lot to her. She called the motel where they had stayed and was told it had not been found. She knew that she had worn it, because she seldom took it off. The next day she returned to work and told her friends what had happened. They sug-gested that she empty out her jewelry box and check, believing that she must have forgotten to take it with her. Although she felt certain that could not have been the case, she emptied the box and checked it on sev-eral occasions; the ring was gone. Five months later, my grandmother's brother died and my parents were on their way to the funeral. Although they were already in the car, my mother decided that she wanted to wear a pin on her dress so she came back into the house and opened her jewelry box. All of her jewelry was pushed aside, and her missing ring was resting there in the center, pushed so hard into the velvet that it left a distinctive mark. My sister and I were flabbergasted! After that happened, we sometimes talked about it and wondered if it had been the work of grandmother.

Entry #6 (Fall 1967)

A sizeable, white wisp that was shaped like a Hershey's Kiss, appeared in the corner of the living room today. The top of it slowly became elongated and then started curling upward toward the ceiling. As the top became longer and thinner, the bottom seemed to decrease in size and volume, and then it disappeared into the ceiling as if it had been sucked up.

It seems that the goings on around here are becoming more and more visible. It's kind of a feeling that "they" have gotten a little more forward or aggressive in "their" dealings with us. We haven't done anything about it, because at this point, we don't know what to do. No one has been hurt, and it doesn't seem like "they" do not intend any particular harm to us or our things. It has always been this way, but I believe that the older I get, the more I seem to notice it. I guess I'll just keep writing about it in the hope that I can get a better handle on things if I can keep track of what is actually happening.

Entry #7 (Fall 1967)

A patch of light appeared on the bedroom wall last night. It was really bright and shaped like a rectangle. The shades were drawn and no light was entering from the window. When we passed our hands over it, there wasn't a shadow. We checked everywhere for a light source, but we found none. There was no patch of light or stream of light leading up to it like there would have been from a spotlight or a projector. We watched it for a good twenty minutes before it just faded away and disappeared. These things we see typically don't just stop abruptly; they usually fade away over some short period of time.

Entry #8 (Winter 1967)

I was just sitting in a chair in the corner of the living room and happened to glance up into the staircase. My bedroom window is in direct line with the door and the reflection of light passes out into the stairwell. During a period of several minutes, a small childlike figure kept passing back and forth. The figure had elongated ears and no particular clothing. It was indistinct in the darkness so I couldn't make out a nose or eyes. There are not any trees on that side of the house, and the windows are all closed now. No one is home but me, and I certainly am not about to go see who it is. As long as it stays there, I'll stay here.

[I often wonder about who or what could be here. All my life I've heard a wide variety of theories from my relatives. There are periods during which things "calm down." Just when we relax and forget for a while what can be going on, something happens again. I suppose it's that feeling of knowing it WILL be back that keeps all of us constantly on edge even when it is not "active." It's a kind of ongoing uncertainty, the looking over your shoulder as you walk through a dark alley feeling. Every time we go through this, there's a break, then it happens again. Mom and Dad have talked for a while about selling this house and moving. I have questions. Does this happen other places a lot? Are they attracted to this place or to the family for some particular reason? Will "they" follow us if we leave?]

Entry #9 (Spring 1968)

Last night we all laid awake listening to a very loud snapping noise. It sounded like the crack of a bull whip, again. The whole house seemed to be filled with it. It came from every corner of every room. There was no rhythm to it, just the random, if constant, snap, snap, snap. We checked the whole house and could not find a source. It finally stopped just before daylight, and we all caught a few minutes of sleep.

Entry #10 (Spring 1968)

Mom and Dad were cleaning the cellar today. Mom was sweeping the corner of the big room and Dad was behind her in another corner. Someone addressed Mom: "Here now! What are you doing?" Startled,

Mom turned around to see who was there. It was a woman's voice that had been quite clear and distinct. No one was there other than her and Dad, and Dad hadn't heard a thing. She answered the invisible voice. She said that it was just a common reaction to answer, even though she knew perfectly well that she and Dad were the only ones down there. There was nothing more.

Entry #11 (Spring 1968)

I washed the dishes last night and they were all fine when I put them in the dish drainer. The silverware was on the bottom. When I dried them, three forks, one knife, and two spoons were bent almost in half. I had been standing right there and didn't hear or see anything unusual, and yet there they were—severely bent. The rest of the things in the silverware section were fine.

[I don't understand what's going on here. Many of things that happened in the past are starting to bother me. Perhaps it's because I am getting older. I'm not really scared because it has always been this way, but I'm starting to wonder what else has happened that I have not been aware of. A "presence" has developed that can be felt—sensed—constantly. I now find it impossible to look the other way. I'm going to just keep writing because I hope that someday by analyzing these events, maybe a pattern will appear that will point toward some answers: to someone who died here, or to someone we knew that can't let go. Any explanation is better than none. Dad doesn't want anyone else involved in this because he is afraid of what people will say, and that it might lower the property value. We don't want a circus going on around here. He believes that everyone will think we're crazy.]

CHAPTER 3

DIARY ENTRIES FROM THE 1970s

"Maybe the time has something to do with all this. I looked at the clock
and it was the same time as my house number."
—DONNA RANDALL FILLIE

Entry #12 (Fall 1971)

I haven't needed to make diary entries lately. Bob and I were married on October 17, 1970, and immediately moved thirty miles away.
Throughout the past year, we visited the house regularly and kept in
touch with the people there. A lot has gone on in the house since I left,
but it is nothing I was able to witness first hand. The little house that we
rented for the last year is "clear," and I certainly have caught up on my
sleep. Next week we are moving back into Mom and Dad's house, but
I'm not expecting that things have changed. Bob has gotten a job back in
town, and I am pregnant. For now it makes sense to save some money,
and also be with my mother because I have really been sick from the
pregnancy.

Entry #13 (Winter 1971)

Bob and Dad went to a meeting this evening and already things are
starting. Mom was sitting in a chair and was visiting with me. Her shoes
were on the floor in front of her. We were discussing the occurrences
that had happened in the house recently and also talking about various
family members. All of a sudden, one of her shoes rolled across the floor.
It stopped for a second, then rolled back toward her foot and stopped.

We just stared at it like a couple of fools. I guess maybe we mentioned that it seemed like someone wanted us to know they were there—as if saying, "Hey, I'm here." As usual, there was nothing threatening about it.

Entry #14 (Winter 1971)

Bob and I were having an argument about a bill that was past due. He was ranting and raving and waving the bill around as he stood over me where I sat on the couch. To break the mood, I tried to tease him by saying that my long deceased grandfather wouldn't appreciate his attitude. Suddenly, the iron ashtray stand slowly leaned in his direction and the large amber ashtray slid out. It glided across the room through the air, then gently lowered onto the rug by my husband's right foot. Well, that certainly shut him up. (Thanks, Grandfather!) I really started to laugh, but then realized that I had just had my first one-to-one connection with some of the unusual things that had happened over the years. It could be family! It could be a protective presence.

Entry #15 (Winter 1971)

Our room is in the old part of the house. Boy, it can get cold out there. Last night we were snuggled in bed under a mountain of blankets when we heard a swishing sound coming down the dark hall toward our room. Rapid footsteps accompanied the noise. Bob and I both sat up and looked toward the sound. It seemed to run down the steps and through the bathroom, right up to the side of our bed. We flinched and put up our arms defensively, because we were sure that, from its obvious runaway momentum, whatever it was would leap right into bed with us. The sound stopped suddenly at the side of the bed near Bob. You should have seen the look on his face when he turned around and looked at me. He was clearly not amused.

I've never seen anything like my husband's attitude. He just dismisses what he sees and hears. He gets angry if I try to discuss it with him. I know he is disturbed by what happens here, but he doesn't want to move. It's an odd situation, because even though I grew up here, I really wouldn't mind moving.

Someone whispered to me last night from the corner of the bedroom. It was a man's voice. I didn't recognize it. It was a whisper, but loud enough that it startled me out of my sleep. There were four or five words, spoken very quickly. The only words I could make out were "down" and "skip." I've thought about what context they could have been in, but it doesn't make any sense to me. Maybe the time has something to do with all this. I looked at the clock and it was the same time as my house number."

[Author's note: In my interviews with Bob, he stated that he simply wanted to believe it all wasn't happening, despite knowing it was—an interesting kind of conscious denial.]

Entry #16 (Spring 1972)

I'm getting so huge from this pregnancy that I can't get comfortable. We have a chair that is S-shaped and is quite comfortable. It presents one major problem, however. Once in it I can't get out of it by myself. I've been sleeping in it quite a lot lately; one more month of this and I'll feel a lot better. Last night—again right at the same time as the house number—I woke up to see something that puzzled me. It didn't scare me, I just couldn't figure out what it was. To my left, there were what looked to be thousands of points of white light. They were in no particular form, but were moving in a swirling motion about five feet off the floor. It kept getting chillier and chillier in the room, so as I watched the lights, I reached for a blanket that was folded at my feet and pulled it up. The light was not coming from any window; the display was in the corner of the dark room. It happened in two different rooms. The lights grew a little brighter, like pinpoints, then gradually faded one by one until the room was dark again.

The house number must hold some significance in all of this. I see it everywhere. Often when I am awakened by something in the night and check the time, it is the same as the house number.

Entry #17 (Spring 1972)

Well, Michelle was born on April 3rd and she's so beautiful. She cries almost constantly, though. I made a nursery for her in one of the back bedrooms. We moved our room next to hers so we will be close by to check in on her.

Entry #18 (Spring 1972)

Last night we heard a man's voice calling for Jenny. First, he said "Jenny?" then "Jen?" I wondered who he was calling for, and from what time frame, since I never knew any Jenny, and when questioned, neither did either one of my parents. Bob and I both heard him calling out. His voice was quiet—hushed—as if he were trying to locate her without disturbing anyone else.

Entry #19 (Spring 1972)

We moved our bedrooms into the other side of the house. The temperature variations were too much for Michelle back there. Today I put her down for a nap in her crib as usual. When I checked on her she was on her back, squealing and giggling with delight. She looked up into the corner of the room, and acted so happy. It's like someone was entertaining her. She seemed completely enthralled with whoever—whatever—it was. It was weird, because I certainly couldn't see anyone, but she certainly could.

I didn't know what to make of it. It seemed odd, but I thought maybe she was just bored. She is a crying baby. She has a sadness about her, so to see and hear her being so happy was wonderful.

Entry #20 (Spring 1972)

Last night, shortly after Bob and I had gone to bed, the door at the other end of the hall creaked open. The house had been quiet up to that point. We looked over our shoulders to the right in response to the noise. As our eyes adjusted to the dim light we both saw a very small being peering around the open doorway into our room from the hall. Its hand was resting on the corner woodwork and it tipped its head as if it were checking on us—looking in on us. It appeared to be the size of a boy, perhaps six or seven years old. I say it looked like a boy only because I didn't see any hair on it. It was definitely a physical being, it had a body with substance to it. The ears were elongated and tipped at the end—the same as I had seen before. He just stood there, and when we didn't react, he pulled his head back and disappeared down the hall. I got up immediately and checked on Michelle. She was sleeping soundly.

[To witness something like this is amazing. It almost seemed like he was checking on us—to make sure we were safe and sound, perhaps. Why aren't we scared? I don't know. I think it may be that there is never enough time to react. It always catches us by complete surprise, and it always happens when we are completely off guard. We just lay there with our mouths open like a couple of dumb fools. By the time that we react, the situation is often over.]

Entry #21 (Spring 1972)

Whoever continues to entertain my daughter is certainly doing a good job. She has stopped most of her constant crying, and seems to be more relaxed. She giggles and laughs through most of her naptime, and no matter when I check on her, she is totally amused by something I cannot see. She has a newly acquired, wonderful smile.

Entry #22 (Spring 1972)

Today a number of strange things happened. For one thing, the electric fan kept turning on by itself. It happened twice even though the switch remained in the off position. Later, Mom and I were watching television and the most ungodly rolling and crashing sound came from the upstairs. It sounded as if a bowling ball was dropped from very high in the air. We hurried up to the second floor to check, but nothing was disturbed anywhere. By then, the noise had stopped. The only unusual thing that we found was that Bob's dresser drawer was pulled all the way out. It had been a very loud, rolling, crashing sound. Mom said that when she was doing the laundry yesterday, she heard something similar upstairs. Nobody else was home at that time. First, she looked up the stairs and Michelle's door was closed. When she checked later, it was open.

[I really don't want my daughter to go through the same things I did while I was growing up here. Bob and I are trying to scrape together enough money to buy a house in the area, and already have looked at a couple of them. If everything wasn't so expensive, it would be a lot easier. Mom and Dad love Michelle so much, so I would like to at least live nearby.]

Entry #23 (Spring 1972)

Mom and Dad were in bed when the flashlight near their bed clicked on. Mom leaned over the side of the bed to check and it clicked off. Later on during the night, something repeatedly pounded up and down the stairs. Diane has made an apartment in the basement for herself and my parents thought it was her for some reason. Dad went all the way downstairs to check, but she was in bed asleep. Both of my parents are really getting fed up with this situation. Mom is funny, she raises her fist and tells them to get lost and go somewhere else. Oh great, get them ticked off at us!

Entry #24 (Spring 1972)

Dad has a number of award plaques on the wall in the living room. During the last few nights, the plaques have been falling off the wall. "They" only focus on his plaques. It is as if they know it gets to him. Pounding is starting in the wall at the foot of the staircase. We keep checking on it, but we can't seem to locate where it's coming from. Dad had the furnace checked out in case it was that, but it's in good condition and nothing is wrong there. Sometimes Bob and I will be in the next room, and Dad will come in to see if we've heard the pounding. We will not have heard a sound—and we were right in the next room.

Entry #25 (Spring 1972)

Today, on my birthday, my friend Colleen came to visit me and to see Michelle. I opened my gift from her as we sat on the couch together talking. Suddenly, the loudest crashing sound I ever heard here in the house filled the room. We both jumped and looked at each other. She looked really scared. The crash sounded like a bowling ball that had been dropped maybe two stories onto a wooden floor. I made a lame excuse about it being something outside, but I could tell that she didn't believe me. I think I acted too casual about it.

[Nothing had actually fallen when we inspected for damage later. It was apparently just the sound. A neighbor came to visit and reported that she had great difficulty breathing in the living room. She would fidget and look distressed. She just couldn't sit in there. It wasn't allergies, she had dogs and cats herself. She commented that she felt "uneasy." Those things suggest it is not just "family" who can perceive the goings on.]

Entry #26 (Spring 1972)

I was just sitting on the couch watching television. I was wearing a silver chain on my left wrist. I was interested in the program, but kept feeling something weird—something crawling—on my wrist. I swatted at it a couple of times and then noticed that the chain was rolling up and down my wrist. Whatever was doing it was on the outside of the wrist and the chain was sort of indented as if a finger was pressed against it.

It repeated all of that several times. I kept my wrist perfectly still as I watched. There was no sound accompanying it. I just felt and saw it rolling.

Entry #27 (Spring 1972)

I was getting ready for bed and as I walked past the closed door to the spare room upstairs, I heard gasping coming from the other side. The height of the sound was a little taller than I was. It sounded like labored breathing. I wasn't about to open the door and see what was on the other side.

[Years later, Lorraine Warren heard that same sound upstairs in the bedroom. Grandfather had emphysema. Could it have been him?]

Entry #28 (Spring 1972)

Throughout the night, Mom heard a group of women chatting in the hall outside of my parents' bedroom door. She tried to make out what they were saying, but she said it sounded like people talking at a large party, and the voices all talked over the top of each other making them all flow together as a single sound. Today we heard music coming from the cellar. (The apartment is gone because Diane moved.) It was the song "Mountain Laurel Time." We have a windup record player and that is one of the records we have. Upon investigating, no one was down there. The record remained in its jacket.

Entry #29 (Summer 1972)

Chanting filled the house all night long. It was maddening!!! No particular tune, very weak, but it played over and over and over.

Entry #30 (Summer 1972)

This was a really strange happening. Today Bob called from work and asked me to buy him a pack of cigarettes. He was totally broke, and didn't have enough money even for coffee break. When he arrived at home his face was white as a—well, white as a ghost. While he was driving home, he stopped at a red light. As he applied the brake, mountains of change fell from the ceiling of his car and landed all over him. Coins went down his shirt, and onto the seat and the floor of his car. He pulled over to the side of the road. While he composed himself, he checked the ceiling and sun visor. There was no possible way that money could have been tucked into the interior of the car ceiling. He gathered up the change and drove on to the store. He had enough change to purchase what he needed and even had some left over for the next day. It was as if someone had overheard and fulfilled his need.

[I see a connection between a situation like this and my grandfather. He was one of the most generous people I knew. If we wanted it and he could provide it, he did. During the depression he owned a dairy farm and would give milk away to families who needed help. Now I feel a little easier. It probably is him or someone like him who means no harm. For some reason they just can't—or don't want to—leave this place.]

Entry #31 (Summer 1972)

I was just in Michelle's room. Sitting on her windowsill is a little wooden sign with her name on it. On the floor under the window she has a large ceramic unicorn. Just now, the left side of the sign lifted up and then set back down. Then the right side lifted and set back down. The whole sign then lifted up, jumped off the windowsill, flipped over, and hit the horn of the unicorn. The horn broke off, rolled over and spun around, and ended up pointing directly at me. It was really freaky. It gave me the chills since it was as if someone was intentionally pointing at me.

Entry #32 (Summer 1972)

Wow. Two days in a row. I wonder why this is happening more frequently. I was carrying a load of clothes into the bathroom to wash and a voice from behind me asked, "What are you doing?" Before I realized that no one was actually there I replied, "I'm just going to wash these clothes." It was a moment later that my hair stood on end and I totally freaked out. Are they that concerned about daily chores? Now I find it hard to take a shower, wondering if they are there watching when I'm naked.

Entry #33 (Summer 1972)

The explosive booming sound is becoming more frequent. Sometimes it sounds like it is way off in another corner of the house. The sounds aren't sharp, but they are quite loud. My mother has very discreetly questioned the neighbors about the sounds, but not one of them reported ever hearing a thing outside. Most of those people are retired and older, so are home when the sound occurs. The events are usually composed of a series of booms, not in any particular timeframe or tempo. There will be one, then another. Then maybe a minute or two will pass, then three or so will sound in close order. Sometimes they actually shake the whole house. Some of our pictures have been knocked off the walls, and others have been jiggled crooked. A couple of weeks ago Mom, Dad, and I were talking about the events. We were seriously discussing what to do about it. None of us are really afraid for our physical safety, but the psychological toll is beginning to be there. Michelle seems happy, but I don't know what effect this will have on her. We are all normal people. I hear so many stories about hauntings. Our particular situation is so bizarre and in many ways different from the others. There is no pattern, here. No rhyme or reason to it. No one jumps out and says, "Boo!" No rattling chains here!

Entry #34 (Summer 1972)

My husband's gold cufflinks are missing from his jewelry box. He hasn't ever worn them. I just have to wonder if something took them. We'll have to wait and see if they show up the way other pieces of jewelry have returned.

Entry #35 (Fall 1972)

The spoons in the dish drainer were bent in half again tonight. I wonder what that is supposed to mean. I probably shouldn't even think this, but if something is trying to give us a message, why isn't it clearer? Now, I don't want anything bad to show up, but these subtle gestures can really drive a person crazy. I mean really, bent spoons? I have tried and tried to figure out what that is supposed to mean. Mom and Dad and I talk on and on about it, but no pattern is there. The thing that has happened most frequently is the apparent obsession with jewelry. Bob is too busy to worry about it. If it happens to him directly he takes notice of it. He won't discuss it, though.

Entry #36 (Fall 1972)

Pat was here watching television with me. All of a sudden there were four loud bangs from the cellar. They were so loud that the floor vibrated. She jumped to her feet from the couch where she had been sitting and just looked at me, clearly frightened. I felt really stupid, but I just pretended that I didn't hear or feel them. I mean, what would I say? "Excuse me, it's just those darn old ghosts playin' around again. Pay them no mind."

Entry #37 (Fall 1972)

Last night, and on a few occasions before then, the hall door by our bedroom creaked open and then closed. It has been doing that so frequently lately that Bob and I now announce, "Come in." Finally, for peace of mind, we put a latch on the door. That seems to have solved it.

Entry #38 (Winter 1972)

Last night something kept lifting the blankets off my shoulders, very gently pulling them down. I pulled them back up over me. It repeated over and over. Finally, I sat up really quick expecting to catch Bob teasing me. There he lay with his back to me, sound asleep with both arms and hands completely under the blankets. He hadn't had time to resume that position without my knowledge.

Entry #39 (Winter 1972)

Today I cleaned the living room, and vacuumed the rug thoroughly. On my way into the kitchen I felt something stuck on my toe. I lifted it to look and found it was my little diamond baby ring. Since I had just finished cleaning the rug it should have been sucked it up. The ring had been in my jewelry box the day before, and to my knowledge, no one had a reason to take it out.

Entry #40 (Winter 1972)

I was just in the kitchen cooking supper and there was a blue hairbrush on the counter, at the back. All of a sudden, it slid clear across the counter and stopped with the handle hanging over the edge. It was just balancing there. I stared at it for a moment, then replaced it to where it belonged. After that, I shook the counter on purpose to see if the brush would slide. It didn't.

[I think that more and more, things are happening mostly just to the women of the household. Dad and Bob haven't reported as many things going on, where Mom and I seem to be more involved. We still can't get a pattern on any of this. Moving the jewelry seems to be a constant thing around here, now. Nothing unusual has been going on in our lives. In fact, everything seems to be going along very well.]

Entry #41 (Spring 1973)

After a relatively quiet period, "they" seem to be back in good form. Last night at 11:15, Bob and I had just gone to bed when the light in the living room downstairs clicked on. We thought that Dad had gone in to check the thermostat because we noticed that the furnace came on. When I called down no one answered, so I got up and checked. The door between the two sides of the house was closed and no one was up. I turned the light off and went back to bed.

[What this type of situation does is make us lie awake night after night just waiting for the next something to happen. Although it could be much worse, and who knows if it may be someday, what really wears on us the most is the element of surprise. It happens on a fairly regular basis, but with no pattern and no predictable time line or schedule.]

Entry #42 (Spring 1973)

This is strange. Well most everything around here is strange, but this puzzled me more than many of the other occurrences. I hate to hear part of something, but not all of it. Last night when we were in bed, someone whispered, "Judge-Ja." It came from between us and toward the bottom of the bed. Aside from the improbability of the event, it made no sense. The voice wasn't male or female. It was really loud and was kind of a coarse whisper. Unnerving to say the least.

Entry #43 (Spring 1973)

Casper the Ghost did an appearing act on the large seascape in Mom and Dad's den. Diane was here and saw it, too. Pure white light in the shape of a ghost. How corny does that sound? It appeared in the top left corner and swirled downward toward the bottom. It almost faded away then reappeared, very brightly. When it finally faded away for good, it left a darkened area on the painting for a few minutes. OK, is that what we're supposed to think "you guys" really look like?

Entry #44 (Spring 1973)

Little strange things again. Pat, Bob, and I watched the bathroom door open and then close and then open again. It's been raining and the windows were closed so there was no breeze coming through them. Earlier, Michelle had been in there brushing her teeth and the light kept clicking on and off. It was not like when the power does it. Each time it was accompanied by a definite click clearly coming from the lamp switch.

[To actually see and hear things like this are totally amazing. It happens right in front of us. I'm starting to think that "something" is trying to relay some message to us. Either we are really stupid or this is far more difficult to untangle than we assumed it would. There is absolutely no reason that we can determine why all of this keeps happening. I really have to laugh when someone is on TV talking about their haunted houses. Not because I don't believe them, but usually they hear a voice and leave the house in screaming fits. By comparison, here, we are living in a little piece of heaven and we haven't gotten to that point yet. I have a feeling that this has been going on for so long it has become normal. Sometimes things happen here that don't get recorded because I need to get ready to go out for dinner or bowling. I must remember to be more diligent in this diary. After all, maybe something will be more important than I think. Are these just friendly "hellos," or is it something more— like that message I indicated? To me, it stands as proof that there is way more out there than what we see. I still can't understand why everything remains so vague.]

Entry #45 (Summer 1973)

I woke up in the middle of the night feeling very disoriented and confused. I was lying on my back with my arms folded up on either side of my head. I went to roll over, but my right wrist and shoulder were pinned to the bed. I literally could not move my wrist off the bed no matter how hard I tried. I couldn't feel or see what was holding it down, but it absolutely would not release my wrist. I kicked my left leg over to try to wake Bob up, but I couldn't reach him. Suddenly, it just released very quickly. I put the light on and told Bob what happened.

[I really don't like this. I can't shake the feeling. Why is something touching me? What was "it" trying to do? Perhaps, nothing more than control me for a moment. I don't know what to think. "It" didn't hurt me, but the thought that I was being restrained, helpless, really troubles me. If at any time Michelle tells me that something similar has happened to her, we're out of here. Even if we have no place to go, I won't have my daughter touched. I am more and more convinced that there is no solution to this. How on earth can we deal with something that we can't see and that so regularly catches us off guard? Sitting up all night is no solution. I'm so exhausted that I can hardly function. I don't know where to turn because Dad has a fit if we even mention it. I don't understand what the big deal would be if someone outside the family knew—especially if they might be able to suggest answers or possible explanations for us. It's like he is obsessed with the secrecy of this thing—as if it will in some way reflect badly on him or the family.]

Entry #46 (Summer 1973)

I had lit a candle on the TV and then went to get a cup of coffee. When I came back into the room, the candle on the old radio was also lit. I asked Bob if he lit it, but obviously not because he was up on a ladder the whole time I was gone. Who did? We were the only ones home tonight.

Entry #47 (Summer 1973)

As I sat in the chair, something kept stroking the back of my hair. It was so gentle. I repeatedly put my hand up to the back of my head and felt around. It continued for a long time. There were distinctive stroke from top to bottom. There was nothing physical there to deliver them. An ice cold breeze blew at the back of my head. There was no use turning around, because from experience, I knew there would be no one there. Had it been offering affection? Was it trying to scare me? Did it have no intention whatsoever beyond the simple acts themselves?

Entry #48 (Summer 1973)

You'd think that after all these years, this would stop (at least I've always hoped it would). When the minister came by yesterday we had him bless the house. I don't believe it did any good because something is still constantly picking at my hair. I have to wonder, when we are all gone from this house will this still be going on? The TV keeps clicking off. Are "they" doing this on purpose, or do "they" think about it and plan it? Perhaps it is better to just accept it all and live with it. Trying to figure it out seems to be driving me toward madness. I've noticed lately that no one wants to be the last person awake at night. If you are, then you can't sleep because you wonder if you're the last person awake. If I happen to wake up in the middle of the night, I lay there and sweat in a quietly hysterical manner. Bob sleeps well through the night. 'They' seem to be leaving him alone. Besides, he's at work most of the time and no matter what he sees or hears he won't discuss it. Men! Husbands!! Bob!!!

Entry #49 (Fall 1973)

There have been loud bangs coming from the left side of our bedroom at the foot of the bed. Bob has checked the spot repeatedly and found nothing. He gets really riled up over it, more because he hates to keep getting out of bed than about the problem itself.

[I'm so tired. Michelle has stopped sleeping as well as before, but she hasn't complained about anything specific. She is healthy and beautiful, but has been a crying child since the second she was born. Sometimes she seems to be very sad. That surprises me since she is the apple of everyone's' eye. She isn't spoiled, but she's very well loved.]

Entry #50 (Fall 1973)

It isn't unusual for a shade in this house to suddenly fly up. They are old and need to be replaced. Lately though, they not only fly up, but then they come back down and then go back up. I would think that something visible would be doing this, but as usual, no one is there but the person who is surprised by it.

Entry #51 (Winter 1973)

Michelle woke us up last night calling loudly from her room. She said that a lady was looking at her. She acted scared, but said that the lady didn't act mad. She was smiling at her, and was up over her head. It's hard to get a description of someone from a child at her age, but she did pretty well. The woman, according to the description we got, had on a blue dress with white spots and a white collar. She had gray hair, either put up in braids or a bun. Michelle said that when she started yelling, the woman simply disappeared.

[I don't feel that Michelle was in any danger. This is the first time that she has been able to tell us about something like this. This entity seemed pleased, like she was just checking on her. I don't know what to do about this. Dad and Mom own the house and their whole life is involved here. If we had the money to move it would be better, but there is something about this house; it seems like no matter what we do, we end up back here. Mom and Dad moved out when they got married and then moved back here. We did the same thing, and just a while ago, Diane moved back here. It's really strange. It seems impossible to me that there are circumstances that are fixed, that a person would have no control over. It seems that when we are here everything is fine financially and personally, but when we leave, things start to fall apart. It's almost like "they" are saying, "We'll take care of things if you are where we want you to be." Once, a while back, I didn't have money for something that Michelle wanted at the store. I had gone through my pocketbook before I left the house and I knew exactly how much money I had. I needed to get something at the store for dinner. I used what I had and only had about 80 cents left. She begged for something so I went back into my pocketbook to check one last time—more to satisfy her than expecting to find any money. Tucked right inside the flap, was a brand new ten-dollar bill. It definitely had not been there before. Again, it seems that someone asked, and it was given.]

Entry #52 (Winter 1973)

The cat has been acting strangely again. He sits and stares at the ceiling by the front door, and nothing will distract him. When someone enters the room, he watches whatever it is move erratically around the room and then stares directly over that person's head. His eyes and head dart around the room. Dad came in a while ago and we watched "it" apparently go directly over Dad's head, then down the wall rapidly toward the floor. We checked repeatedly for flies, cobwebs, spiders, or anything else that might move, but there is never anything there. It's becoming really creepy. He certainly sees something that we can't.

[Just a note: We check everything possible to make sure that whatever happens around here isn't caused by something that can be explained. Many of the things can be. I'm only writing about the occurrences that have been checked out thoroughly and have remained unexplained.]

Entry #53 (Winter 1973)

Mom and I were just outside for a while and when we came back into the house it smelled heavily of cigar smoke. Neither one of us knows anyone who smokes cigars. Grandpa Horton did, but he's been dead for years. Nothing was disturbed, and besides, we were only out in the front yard for about ten minutes and no one was around. The odor was really, really strong.

[Grandpa Horton never lived in this house, but he did eventually move into the house next door.]

Entry #54 (Winter 1973)

There were a series of loud knocks downstairs. Bob and I heard two separate sets. They sounded like they were coming from the foot of the stairs in the living room. Bob took the flashlight and investigated. The whole house was quiet. Everyone else was asleep except Michelle who was crying loudly. So I brought her to bed with us for the night.

Entry #55 (Winter 1973)

Just since Christmas there is a new, weird, all pervasive feeling in the house. No one sleeps very well. It's like something is going on that we don't know about. We all carry a frantic feeling, but nothing is wrong here with us. The feeling is one of uneasy anticipation—dread; like you feel something is about to happen—expecting all heck to break loose. Interestingly, the unsettling feeling is not just confined to the members of our household. We've listened to a number of neighbors who all relate they feel anxious and have not been sleeping well during the exact same period of time.

Entry #56 (Winter 1973)

Mom's flashlight clicked on again last night, and when she looked over the edge of the bed, it clicked off by itself.

Entry #57 (Spring 1974)

While tucking Michelle in tonight, it looked like someone sat on the edge of her bed, then got up, and sat back down again. The whole edge of the bed dipped down fairly far. No one else was in the room. I put her into bed between Bob and me. She thinks it's a real treat to sleep with us. Maybe she will sleep with us tomorrow night, too.

Entry #58 (Summer 1974)

Michelle is downstairs crying. She said that someone tried to talk to her—up close. When she ran out of her room, ice cold air blew against her back.

[I don't want to scare her. I don't know what to do. Bob has started to get really mad if anyone mentions these things that continue happening. Michelle still doesn't seem like any of this is affecting her beyond the moment. She goes to sleep, and doesn't act like she's afraid to go anywhere in the house. It's strange, but she gets upset when something wakes her up but then she's fine about it later on.]

Entry #59 (Fall 1974)

[Thought I would take this time to try to connect some of the things that I have been writing about. A lot of the things that happen are repetitive. I hate to keep writing about the same things over and over. I suppose that some of the things have gotten by me because I sometimes have things to do that have to come first. We went to hear a lecture at UCONN by Ed and Lorraine Warren: the ghost hunters. I wanted to see if what they know is similar to what has been going on around here. They seemed to talk a lot about demons and it scared the daylights out of me. I listened really carefully to try to determine if any of their experiences were like what we have. Some of what they said seemed to pertain to our situation. Lots of times it gets extremely cold in here. I guess it could be, like they said, that a spirit would need energy in order to materialize. I still think that this must be someone who is familiar with this house and with us. Ed and Lorraine believe that these type of ghosts aren't harmful, which matches our experiences. Given a choice between a demon and a friendly spirit, I'd choose the spirit every time. What has happened to Michelle would indicate that our "visitors" were once human. She knew that the "person" visiting her was my grandfather. An adult may be tricked because they would have a preconceived notion of what he would look like. But for a child of that age, there would be no point to it. I really wanted to ask some questions, but that would have alerted everybody to our situation and Dad would have been more than a little upset. I also felt that the Warrens would have insisted on knowing where the house was. I would love to be able to ignore all of this, but I have been writing about it for so long that I feel compelled to continue. I won't call it an obsession, but I keep hoping that somehow it will come to be easier to understand. I'm not sure how understanding it will help me do anything about it.]

Entry #60 (Winter 1974)

Michelle went to get into bed tonight and her mattress was soaking wet. I would have thought that she wet her bed, but it was at the bottom. When I made the bed this morning, nothing seemed wrong. The odd thing is that the sheet was dry, the blankets were dry, and the bedspread was dry. There was no wet spot on the ceiling from where water could have leaked. I cleaned the spot anyway and then remade the bed.

Entry #61 (Winter 1974)

The weirdest thing just happened (surprise, surprise!). Michelle just came into the bathroom with a jar of marbles. She wanted to know where the toy ring came from. I looked in the jar and my baby ring was balanced on top of the marbles. The ring had been in my jewelry box since the toe incident and I was certain that it had not been removed. Before I had gone into the bathroom, I had picked up all the toys. I put the marbles into the jar, and my ring was not with them. It had to have been put on top of the marbles after I had put them into the jar.

[Author's note: Donna put the ring back into her jewelry box. Years later, when Dale was born in 2007, Donna was going to give the ring to Michelle to give to Dale. The ring was gone. It has never been seen again since this writing.]

Entry #62 (Winter 1974)

Michelle called out again. Her light had gone on and off repeatedly. I went in to see what was going on, and something was tapping on the outside of her window. Her shade was down. The tapping was loud. It moved from top to bottom, one tap, a series of five, one tap, a series of five. Her room is on the third floor so I knew that no one could have been doing it from the outside. I called Bob, but he didn't believe me.

[It seems at this time that we have a "conquer and divide" situation brewing. That in itself is very uncomfortable—and new and different. Things keep happening around here even though Dad hasn't seemed to experience much of it lately. The men seem to be less absorbed with the household and these goings on. Less is happening to Mom, although she still occasionally hears women's voices outside of her door at night. I don't understand it. Why do "they" change the object of "their" attentiveness? Maybe the men are less receptive or maybe they have been more willing to denounce what has been going on. In any case, I have begun to realize the amount of entries in this diary are coming more and more often. In going over them, I still see no pattern—except the jewelry of course.

Entry #63 (Winter 1974)

Happy B-day Mom!

Entry #64 (Winter 1974)

It felt like someone had their finger on the back of my neck, and was rolling my silver chain up and down. What the heck is it with the jewelry? I wonder if there is something that was lost on the property or in the house. Nothing has been found so far, but this certainly is a large place, and there is an attic over the old bedrooms that is stuffed with hay. I don't know if anyone has been up there recently. When I was little my bed was right under the hatch, but I never thought about what was up there. I'm really curious, but not ready to go up there to investigate yet. I asked Dad and he said that there's just a bunch of old paper and boxes and stuff. Maybe that area should be cleaned out before it catches on fire.

Entry #65 (Winter 1974)

Last night it was back to the old light clicking on and off. If I could be sure it would go back off, I wouldn't have to keep getting out of bed.

Entry #66 (Spring 1975)

Dad just came in from the garage and announced that he had seen Grandpa George standing over in the corner looking at him.

I was surprised that he didn't seem upset. Dad said that he just stood there looking at him and had a pleased look on his face. He was wearing a plaid flannel shirt and baggy jeans. The fact that he actually saw the spirit of a person and didn't even get ruffled was fully out of character, but certainly welcome. This is a very important development to me. It seems possible that this could be who has been around here. I'm not sure if he is the only one though, because some of the pranks like the bent spoons and cigar smoke wouldn't follow his personality. And, there is the little boy and the old woman. I wonder what I would do if I saw him? I don't think that I would have stood there very long. But when I really think about it, if it is Grandpa, I wasn't afraid of him when he was alive, was I?

Entry #67 (Summer 1975)

I just brushed my teeth before going to bed and I noticed the curtain by the vanity moving back and forth. I looked over to see what it was, and Michelle's little black cowboy boots were sitting on the floor just under the curtains. The right boot was lying over on its side, but then stood back upright. It continued that activity for some time—lying on its side and then standing up again. For some reason the playfulness of it all made me smile.

Entry #68 (Winter 1975)

When Mom, Dad, and I came back from the store today the whole house smelled like cigar smoke. As before, it was really strong. Everything was closed up tight and no one had been in here.

Entry #69 (Winter 1975)

We have had a relatively quiet time here at the house lately. I don't understand why, but it is great. I know I have relaxed a good deal and it appears the others have as well. Everything is going along well with all of us. Bob has a good job, and I have started working part-time. I wonder if, because we are outside so much and away from the house, the "events" are just less noticeable.

Entry #70 (Spring 1976)

Are our children really ours? I know that's a strange question, but as I grow older I have come to question a lot of things. These things that happen in this house are way beyond reason. This newest series of things from Michelle is really getting to me. Mom was cleaning out the hutch today and was going through old photos of family. She picked up a picture of my grandfather and asked Michelle if she knew who it was. Michelle became very excited and started smiling. She said, "Yes, it's George. He used to come see me in my crib when I was a baby." She had not seen a picture of him before because we are not the photo-on-the-wall kind of people. The photos that we have are taken out once in a while, but to my knowledge, she had never seen a picture of him before. She certainly didn't have any way of knowing his name.

[I think this makes me feel somewhat better; I mean at least we're not dealing with some creature of the night with red eyes. But still, who was the boy in the doorway a while ago? And why would Grandpa be taking jewelry? And I wonder what we experience before we are born. What residual information is left in us? What was in OUR heads that we don't remember now?]

Entry #71 (Summer 1976)

My second child is due in February. I can't wait!

Entry #72 (Winter 1976)

I have lived with all of this since childhood so, beyond being startled, I almost never have any sort of serious reaction. Fear is not a big part of it. It has always just been more of an irritation or distraction. However, I heard something today that just about put me over the edge. I still can't believe it! I will never, ever, be able to explain what occurred. Just writing it down gives me prickly skin and chills that make my teeth chatter. I'm almost afraid to write about it for fear someone will accuse me of going off the deep end, but, for the record, here goes. Michelle was in the car with me today on our way home from the store. I was talking to her and she was sitting there very quietly. All of a sudden, she looked at me very thoughtfully and I swear to God, said, "You know, when I was older, I was walking on this road, and a car came from behind and hit me. Then I went up to see the man and he said, 'No little boy, you have to go back.' So, I came back and then I was your baby." Then she just settled back and acted like she had before. I almost drove off the road. I had to stop and collect myself. The hair on the back of my neck stood up and I got chills from my feet to my head. Upon writing this down, I still can't believe it. All of those disturbing feelings return. For her it was a fully matter-of-fact observation—a memory she wanted to share about an occurrence she clearly felt was in no way out of the ordinary. She continues to act normal in every way. It actually scared me—something more than disturbing me but I suppose less than terrifying me. I don't believe in reincarnation, but at her age why would she say something like that? She is too young to make up such a story. What freaked me out the most was the tone of her voice. It sounded very old and mature, distant, perhaps—well-constructed and was in no way disconcerting to her. She had certainly never witnessed such an experience nor can I believe that she could have ever heard such a story being related. I was shocked to the point of sweaty palms and a distressing, light-headed, adrenalin rush. I told my husband and my mother. They listened with wide eyes and open mouths.

[On another occasion only a few weeks later something prompted a somewhat similar incident. Michelle looked around as if suddenly finding herself in unfamiliar surroundings. She looked up at me and said, "I was starving and walking and I went to a house and the lady said, 'No, little boy, I have no food, I can't feed you.' She appeared quite serious and her voice took on that same distant tone as before. It was as if the story popped into her head and she just had to tell me. I never talked to her about it. She wasn't one for making things up. During the relating of both stories there was an automated quality in the presentations, like from the memory to the tongue with no thinking intervening.]

Entry #73 (Winter 1977)

I guess regardless of what goes on around here, unless it's really spectacular, I have to stop writing for a while. I'm getting jumpy about my pregnancy because it's getting so close. When I can, I'll start again.

Entry #74 (Winter 1977)

Well, we have a gorgeous baby boy named Bob. He has a sparkling personality and smiles a lot. Gotta love him, he's so darn cute! I couldn't be happier. Michelle took one look at him and said, "I don't want him, put him back." I don't think so!

Entry #75 (Winter 1977)

I have to go into NY today so I just went out to see if Mom and Dad were up yet. I heard low talking, giggles, and laughing coming from the den. Nobody was there, but the sounds didn't stop as I entered the room. The lights and TV were turned off and the dog was sleeping in front of the fireplace. Mom and Dad were still asleep in their room. The noise was located near the top of the cellar stairs and continued for a few minutes before fading away. I purposely stood there for a little while, just to see if it would begin again. After the voices faded out completely, the house was so still that it took on an eerie feeling.

Entry #76 (Winter 1977)

I was just upstairs sitting on the bed in our room and I noticed shadows flickering back and forth on the door. Whatever light source was casting the shadows would have had to have been in the room with me. The dog roused for a moment, lifted its head, and looked toward the door. The shadows were not distinct, so I couldn't tell if they represented anything in particular. They were small though, about the size of a cat. Lots of them, maybe six or seven. The hair stood up on the back of my neck. What were they?

Entry #77 (Spring 1978)

The edge of Michelle's mattress lowered repeatedly, as if someone was sitting on it. She told me that a man visited her. He had on a tall black hat and "funny old clothes. When she called out to me, he turned away and just disappeared in the hallway." I had of course just come that way and there was nothing unusual out in the hall.

Entry #78 (Summer 1978)

An odd thing happened today. It is extremely hot outside, and the furnace came on. A minute or two later, the whole side door of the furnace blew off. It slammed into the cellar wall and made a terrible noise. Everyone ran downstairs to see what it was. The thermostat was off, so Dad called the repairman and he didn't have a clue why it would do such a thing. He just stood there scratching his head. In the summer we flip the switch at the top of the cellar stairs because it shuts down everything in the cellar since there's no reason to have the furnace on.

Entry #79 (Fall 1978)

I don't understand why all of this keeps happening. (How many times have I said that in these pages?) Recently, we have made some new friends. As soon as we got close to them I broached the subject of haunted houses. I still haven't mentioned anything about this house, but I brought it up in general terms. I realized that there are a lot of these situations going on in this immediate area. Most people just live with it. They are afraid to say anything because if they need to sell their homes no one will buy them. Lately though, I've been seeing some of "these kinds of homes" for sale. Interestingly, certain people feel really privileged to live in them. I guess that is the situation here. Dad has everything he owns tied up in this property. As he gets older, he's becoming nervous about being able to support it all. Anyway, these people we met from Litchfield have a similar problem, but it involves a clock that chimes on the very second at the time the former owner died. We've only had one death in this house that I know of. My great-grandmother died in her apartment in the cellar. It seems that I had a life-threatening illness when I was about four months old. She told my mother that she had lived a long life, and that if I could be spared, she would gladly die instead of me. The day that my parents found out that I was going to live, my mother went downstairs to tell my great-grandmother. Within the hour, she sat down in her rocking chair and died. Sometimes I feel guilty about that. I mean, I'm honored but I feel like she sacrificed herself for me.

[That was Minnie Gray. My maternal great-grandmother. She's the one who took my grandmother in after she was left on a doorstep. She also took my grandfather from the Gilbert Home Orphanage in Winsted.]

Entry #80 (Fall 1978)

Last night while I was trying to fall asleep, something kept stroking my hair again. I was facing Bob with my back to the wall. It kept stroking and stroking until I put my hand on the back of my head. As soon as I took my hand away, it started again. Then, very gently, my silver chain started to roll up and down the back of my neck. I can never feel a finger, it just seems to be a whisper of pressure. Of course, as soon as I put my hand there, it stopped. It seems to be some sort of a game—at least from the perpetrator's point of view. When things of that nature are going on, I don't feel like I need to be afraid, because I get the impression that whoever is doing it is purposefully doing it very gently. It certainly is disconcerting though.

Entry #81 (Fall 1978)

Today I got to thinking about the cufflinks that were lifted from Bob's jewelry box. We had quite a discussion about the situation. I decided to look again just for the heck of it so I went upstairs to check. Well, there they were, everything was pushed aside and they were sitting right there in the middle. I came running downstairs to tell Mom because I couldn't believe it. I had to pick Michelle up from a birthday party, so I decided that I'd take the cufflinks with me. All the way home I let Michelle hold them in her hand, and her hand was in her pocket. When I unlocked the front door, Michelle was clinking them around in her pocket, but when she pulled her arm out of her coat sleeve, they were gone. "Here we go again," was my first reaction. We retraced our steps, and out in the driveway by the side of the car we spotted the cufflinks. But, they were point down, side by side, like someone had driven over them, or walked over them. No way was that possible when she had gotten all the way into the house with them in her hand. It's like someone just whisked them away in a split second. When Bob came home, he was totally amazed at what had happened.

Entry #82 (Winter 1978)

I came upstairs to bed and stepped out into the hallway to ask if Bob would turn the heat down, and something brushed by me. It was like a pressure that pushed against me on my right side. It wasn't solid, because it looked like nothing was even there, but it trailed a breeze behind it. It went directly into the spare room over the hall. I don't know what it was, but I could "feel" it.

Entry #83 (Winter 1978)

Mom's diamond ring has been returned to her jewelry box after having been missing for two days. She had checked every day just to make sure it really wasn't there.

Entry #84 (Winter 1978)

Today something happened that made me stop and think. I had to go to the store, so I left the kids with Mom because it is really cold. I got to the top of the hill, and the whole car filled with the smell of cigar smoke. It was really noticeable, and really strong. I slowed down because I couldn't understand why it had suddenly appeared. When I got to the top of the next hill, I slowed down even more, and went to apply my brakes. I had almost none! That was the first time something like that had ever happened to me. I had just enough brake left to eventually bring my car to a stop at the side of the road. I walked to a house and called Mom to let her know what had happened. Someone was warning me! They probably saved my life, because at the bottom of that hill are two S curves that were dangerously iced over. I don't understand why they may now be following us out of the house, but I'm eternally thankful that they did on that occasion. It reminded me of a story told about my grandmother who was driving home one night alone in the car. Suddenly she heard a baby crying in the back seat. She immediately pulled over and stopped, but when she checked, of course there was nothing there.

[My mother had to pull over several times. When she came home, she expressed how upset she was about it.]

Entry #85 (Spring 1979)

Michelle informed me this morning that someone was "feeling" her hair last night. I asked her what she meant and she said that her bed was shaking and someone was "feeling her hair." She indicated that she thought I was checking on her so it didn't bother her at the time. It appears that the whole family is being checked on at night.

Entry #86 (Spring 1979)

Michelle is extremely upset today. She dreamed all night that her brother had been severely injured. Today, his battery-operated dog kept turning on by itself. It occurred a half dozen times or so, until I removed the battery. I don't think it was anything ghostly, but I mean to keep a very close eye on him anyway.

Entry #87 (Spring 1979)

This is kind of a strange thing. Last week, Mom opened her mailbox by the front door and there was a note in it from two old friends. It said "Sorry we missed you—Betty and Fred." The only people she knows by that name are Betty and Fred Wilcox. She hadn't seen them in nearly 30 years, and said she'd have to locate their number and call them. She was clearly upset that she had missed them. The writing on the note was in pencil and very shaky. The pencil had been pressed down really hard onto the paper. When she called them they were very surprised to hear from her. They said they had not stopped by and didn't leave a note. In fact, they have not been in the area for years.

Today she got a note from Ruby and Garnet. It was almost the same writing—sort of shaky and pressed deeply into the paper. She had not seen them in many years and commented that she would call them and have them over for lunch. That afternoon, they appeared at the door. Mom welcomed them in, and told them that she had gotten their note and was sorry that she had missed them. They looked at each other clearly puzzled, then looked at her and told her that they had not left a note. They hadn't stopped, and, in fact, had just decided to do so a few minutes before. They no longer live in the area, and it was an unplanned stop as they were just passing through.

Entry #88 (Summer 1979)

Skippy and I were on the bed in my room just a little while ago, and I was reading while he was sleeping. All of a sudden, he jumped up as if someone had awakened him, abruptly. He was very alert and excited. He watched as someone (I presume) came in through the door and crossed the room. He looked upward, his head and eyes following whatever it was, past the bed and over to the far wall. He acted really happy to see whoever it was. His front paws were dancing up and down a mile a minute, and he was making little hello sounds in his throat. I saw nothing there. As soon as "it" left the room Skippy laid down and went to back to sleep.

Entry #89 (Summer 1979)

Skippy was at it again, but this time he didn't seem quite so happy to see whoever was here. I watched Skippy cower at the foot of the stairs. His tail was tucked up underneath his belly and his body language indicated that someone or something was reaching down the stairs to him. It looked like he wasn't quite sure if whatever it was would be friendly or not. He made it almost all the way to the floor, then gradually stood up, put one foot on the bottom step, then stretched his neck out, as if he was sniffing at an invisible hand. He really reacted to something, like he wasn't sure at first, but then decided it was okay after all.

[I wonder if animals can see what it is that is here. They react as if they can. I guess we won't ever know. I wish I could see what they see.]

Entry #90 (Summer 1979)

(Night time) Michelle was downstairs crying just now. She said that someone had tried to talk to her, up very close near her ear. She got so scared that she couldn't call us, so she ran out of her room and down the stairs. About halfway down, ice cold air blew against her back. She finally calmed down, so I'm going to sleep with her the rest of the night. It was an unusual reaction for her—being frightened.

[What is really strange is the reaction to a situation like this. She seems very upset as it's happening, but then is fine a very short while afterward. Also, she doesn't even seem to want to know what is going on here. She still seems to be totally unafraid to be anywhere in the house by herself.]

Entry #91 (Summer 1979)

We all came home from a fireman's parade to find our porch lights on. Quite a discussion followed because Mom and Dad and the kids were all with us. No one had turned them on before we left.

Entry #92 (Fall 1979)

Mom was trying to sleep last night, but there seemed to be a group of people in the hallway outside of her door talking. As it had once before, it sounded like a gathering of a large number of people and they were all talking at once. She got really ticked off, and told them in no uncertain terms that she wanted to sleep and to please get out. Believe it or not, their voices faded away until it was quiet again. She has just about had it with all this. She's just a feisty Yankee I guess. Clearly, her position is that she owns the house, darn it, and nobody, or no one, will come in here and disturb her. I have to laugh sometimes because she gets so indignant. This morning she asked me if I thought that she was crazy. I prefer to think she isn't, because if she is, then I suppose we all are.

Entry #93 (Fall 1979)

Skippy has been very interested in the corner of the den. He rouses up, growls, and acts very disturbed. There is nothing there that any of us can see. He can't seem to take his eyes off the spot. He has great difficulty calming down afterward. He just keeps jerking his head up and looking. Sometimes he will get up and walk over, then wag his tail at whatever it is. Who knows?

Entry #94 (Fall 1979)

Michelle woke up screaming last night. She was so scared she was practically hysterical. She said that she looked up and a woman was smiling down at her. She described her in detail: older with dark hair pulled back and she wore a necklace and earrings.

As the woman opened her mouth to speak, Michelle panicked and screamed. The woman disappeared. She can sleep with us tonight. That does it, I'm calling the minister.

Entry #95 (Fall 1979)

This is a great one!!! My mother-in-law has been asking if she can come for the weekend. She has a dog that she usually brings, but our dog is aggressive so I worry about a scuffle. She said that she would keep him with her in her room, so there should be no problem. I went to pick her up, and she was excited about coming. We have taken the kids to her house almost every Sunday for years because she doesn't drive, and we wanted them to know each other. Well, she settled into her room and everything seemed fine. We all retired for the evening, and were looking forward to doing some shopping together the next day. The following morning she was miserable. The first thing out of her mouth was, "I want to go home." Concerned that we had done something to offend her, we asked her why. "Someone kept pulling my blankets off all night and I kept pulling them back up." Bob and I looked at each other. Before either of us could give a response she had more to say. "And, the dog kept whining and crying and wouldn't get off of me." We looked at each other again. She continued. "Then, someone was blowing in my face. Pulling off the blankets and blowing in my face again, but nobody was there." We couldn't keep a straight face. I tried, but couldn't. She looked puzzled. My husband said, "Oh, Ma, it was probably the dog." "NO!" she replied rather panicky, "it was a ghost, and I know it."

[At the time that I am transcribing this diary, Bob and I have been married for twenty-nine and one half years. She has never slept at our house since that night. In fact, she will always go home before it gets dark! She has accused us of trying to scare her just so she won't come and visit. How sad, although from her perspective it may be the only "reasonable" explanation.]

Entry #96 (Winter 1979)

Michelle woke up last night to what she described as a very pleasant voice. It was a woman's voice. She apparently said, "I have something to tell you." Michelle said that the whole room was flooded with light. She rolled over slowly, and faced the voice, and saw a very tall woman with her back to Michelle. Her first impression was that it was an angel. She looked like a regular physical person. Michelle, not being an adult, described her as having floor-length hair that was "mixed with gold," and as being "very wavy, and curly." She was wearing "a white and gold robe that went to the floor." Michelle could see that the figure "tipped her head from side to side, like she was thinking about something." Michelle, interested of course, instinctively asked, "What?" The figure said, "I have some business to finish," and just disappeared. Michelle said that it was just like someone turned off a light. She said that she wasn't afraid at all, in fact she was very calm. There had been nothing threatening about it.

CHAPTER 4

DIARY ENTRIES FROM THE 1980S

"I wish I knew what on earth is going on here. Something is definitely wrong here, but no matter what anyone sees or hears, there can be no rational explanation."
—DONNA RANDALL FILLIE

Entry #97 (Spring 1980)

This morning Michelle told me that she couldn't sleep at all because she felt "bothered" by something, but she didn't know what. She kept trying and trying, but she couldn't sleep. She felt that she needed to keep her eyes closed or else she would see "something." Then a very pleasant voice told her to "get the cross." The only cross she has is the one that used to belong to me. She got out of bed, put the cross on, and immediately went to sleep.

Entry #98 (Summer 1980)

For the last two nights in a row Michelle reported that something was stroking her hair. She said that it was not a hand in the human sense, just a gentle stroking. It can be very annoying if you're not in the mood. It's like, "Leave me alone," but it won't.

Entry #99 (Summer 1980)

After arriving home from grocery shopping at 9 p.m. Bob went upstairs and the kids and dog were over in the corner of the living room together. I flopped on the loveseat at the foot of the stairs. My sneakers were on the floor in front of me and to my surprise, one did a complete rollover and ended in an upright position about one and one half feet from where it started. For some reason, it made me smile.

Entry #100 (Fall 1980)

Mom and Dad invited us over for dinner, and Diane came up. We were sitting at the table eating, and the old mantle clock started running and chiming. That clock hasn't worked for years and years. The main spring is broken because it was wound too tightly, but they keep it because it is so old, and is decorative. Well, we all stared at each other with our mouths hanging open. It chimed about seven or eight times and made a sort of grinding noise and came to a stop.

[Michelle still has that clock and it still chimes without the mechanism to this day.]

Entry #101 (Winter 1981)

I was just putting on makeup in the bathroom and the dog kept growling and lifting up his lips like he was very agitated about something. Michelle was in her room upstairs with Bobby and they were playing quietly.

Entry #102 (Winter 1981)

Today I went in to clean Bobby's room and it smelled really strong of cigar smoke. There was no smoky haze or anything, just the really strong smell. Now, I know that there is no possible way on earth that someone was actually smoking a cigar in there. So, do "they" project the scent for some reason? If there's a message there, I'm afraid I missed it.

Entry #103 (Spring 1982)

I wish I knew what on earth is going on here. Something is definitely wrong here, but no matter what anyone sees or hears, there can be no rational explanation. I have spoken many times with the minister and he seems to understand the situation. There is nothing he can say that will change anything. We have had him speak with Michelle and he says that she has developed an attitude of acceptance as if she understands, too.

Why can't we understand it? It's almost impossible to understand how something like this can go on. The house has been blessed, and it still goes on. Mom has demanded that "they" leave, and they do, but only for the time being. "They" don't hurt anyone; "they" aren't even apparently trying to scare anyone. "They" are just here and that is that!

Entry #104 (Summer 1982)

Something had hold of the corner of the sheet on Michelle's bed and kept pulling her toward the bottom corner of the bed. She would almost slide off the bottom, then crawl back up pulling the sheet with her. Over and over again it pulled her toward the edge and she would crawl back up. She started to get really mad about it because she didn't want to be disturbed. It seems that something was playing a little game to see how aggravated it could get her. Rather than being scared, she was just plain mad.

Entry # 105 (Fall 1982)

Little Bob is really a quiet kid, so when he woke us up last night I thought that maybe he was sick. He was crying, and said that someone was calling him, close to his head. When he looked around, no one was there, but they kept on calling and calling his name. What should we do? No one likes when this happens. The kids are happy here, and don't seem to typically be bothered by all of this. Something like what just happened is upsetting as it is going on, but then seems to be forgotten almost immediately.

Entry #106 (Fall 1982)

I was just sitting in the den reading a book and something or someone was stroking the back of my hair. It was very gentle and pleasant. I put my hand on the back of my head. Nothing was there. It kept stroking. It wasn't doing anything seriously scary, just stroking and stroking. I left it alone. It seemed to be enjoying the activity as much as I was.

Entry #107 (Winter 1982)

Michelle's room was full of cigar smoke last night. My pillow smelled like Lysol. Perhaps "spirits" have really poor aim!

[Again I have to wonder why there are these scents in the house. It really irritates me sometimes—less than that they are here because I can't get a grasp on it. Irritated is clearly not the right word. These things keep happening over and over and no adequate explanation develops. Perhaps the feeling is frustration. If we're supposed to figure it out, they better give us some more definitive clues.]

Entry #108 (Winter 1983)

Thank God, things have been very quiet for a long period of time. If only it would stay this way. We're all doing well, and have been able to sleep without wondering what will happen next.

Entry #109 (Summer 1984)

I was home all alone. The phone rang and I picked it up thinking it was just like any random call we get. I couldn't have been more wrong.

I answered and said hello and on the other end there was a commotion. It was as if I was was listening to something happen in real time, but it sounded like it was from a past time by the Victrola-like-sounding voices and noise. Either that, or I thought it was some type of crank call.

After a few moments it became very apparent to me that this was no crank call. It sounded like there was a real disaster in the making going on. There was a voice echoing in what sounded like the distance as he said, "Ahoy matey! Freighter up ahead!" Then I heard men yelling in the background. There was confusion, splashing sounds as if people were abandoning ship, and other sounds typical of an old-time marine emergency. Then the line just went dead and I heard the dial tone. I know in my mind my ears were witnessing a real incident from the past that somehow came through the phone.

Entry #110 (Fall 1984)

The clock is still going strong. Tonight when Michelle came into our room to tell us something, the dog hopped up and ran to the edge of the bed. He wasn't greeting her, but someone behind her. We all looked past Michelle toward where he was looking. Of course, nothing was there even though he gave every indication that there was. His interest continued for some time.

Entry #111 (Winter 1984)

Sounds like someone is banging up and down the stairs. The kids are right here with me and no one is physically there. It's happened two or three times now and the dog keeps looking over there when it happens. Well, have a ball guys, because I'm outta here for now.

Entry # 112 (Winter 1984)

Michelle stayed home from school today, and every time she went into the living room, the pendulum on the antique clock would swing back and forth. It's broken and hasn't worked for years. The main spring is broken, and it's too costly to fix. She never touched it, but it would make a cranking sound, and swing back and forth.

Entry #113 (Spring 1985)

Michelle seems anxious and wants to stay away from her room. She comes into our room in the middle of the night with her pillow, and I have found her sleeping on the floor next to our bed. I think I will have the new minister come for a visit and bless the house again. We talked about moving again, but this time the kids had a fit and wanted to stay here. I don't want any problems to arise from this experience. They say it doesn't bother them, but for goodness sake, if they don't want to stay in their rooms at night, then I know that it does.

Entry #114 (Spring 1985)

We had bought a huge stuffed St. Bernard dog at a flea market. It kept getting in the way so I put it in the spare room over the stairs. Yesterday morning when I got up, it was sitting in the hall outside of my bedroom door. I put it back in the spare room. When I got up this morning, it was again outside of my door. Michelle was still sleeping on both days. I had put a nail in the latch to keep the door to the spare room closed. It is too high for her to reach. I think I'll get rid of the play thing as soon as she forgets that she has it or stops playing with it.

Entry #115 (Summer 1985)

Bob, who hasn't been affected a lot by this, was sitting on the couch at 5 a.m. waiting for us to leave on vacation. (Cape May, New Jersey! Yeah!) Anyway, he jumped up and went running across the room. His eyes grew huge as he looked toward the television. His track trophy had slid across the entire top of the television, then stopped dead in its tracks. The fact that we were leaving for a weeks' vacation helped a lot to stop him from dwelling on it.

[I wonder why these things only happen to one person at a time. It was obviously meant for just Bob to see. Possibly if we were all to see something at once, we may be able to figure this out.]

Entry #116 (Fall 1985)

Michelle asked if her friend Charlene could stay overnight so, all things considered, we said yes. All went well until the middle of the night. Charlene got out of bed and jumped into bed with Michelle, yelling about Michelle keeping her awake all night making animal noises. Michelle kept denying that she was making any noises, but Charlene didn't believe her. Charlene said that there were "creepy noises" coming out of the corner of the room, and that Michelle was "blowing cold air in my face all night long." Her parting shot to Michelle when she left was, "If it wasn't you, than you have a ghost in this big old house."

[The feeling, which we've all had that someone is here with us, was never more evident than when Michelle stayed away from home for the first time. She didn't say much about what she and her friend did, but mentioned that her friend's house was "clear."]

Entry # 117 (Winter 1985)

Much of the same goings on all summer. Nothing dramatic has happened. I didn't get a chance to keep up the journal, because Dad has been very sick, and was hospitalized for quite a while with heart problems. I'll try to be more dedicated to this venture in the future.

Entry #118 (Winter 1985)

Last night there was mist in the living room. It didn't take on any particular form or substance, just a hazy mist close to the floor. I didn't notice it at first, but when I did, the first thing that came to mind was smoke from a fire. There was no smell of smoke in the house and the room was cool. All the doors and windows were closed. It hung close to the floor and just remained a hazy strip.

Entry # 119 (Winter 1985)

Today the mantle clock started chiming on its own. It is clearly still broken.

Entry #120 (Winter 1985)

Bob Jr. stayed home from school today because he has a bad cold. He was watching television and I was sitting on the loveseat sewing a button on his father's shirt. We both watched in amazement as the lamp slid across the table, hovered in mid-air, and smashed onto the floor. Okay, guys, enough is enough. At least you can clean up after yourself!

Entry #121 (Winter 1985)

Bob Jr. has no particular knowledge about the goings-on in the house. With the exception of a few incidences, he has pretty much escaped the situation. He told me today that he was awake most of the night because someone kept shaking his shoulder and patting him on the back. He tried to sleep, but when he did, it would be repeated over and over. He was furious this morning because he thought it was his sister. She was mad at him for accusing her of doing it. The joy of being siblings!

[I didn't try to push him about it, but he was obviously irritated. He said that he heard someone calling him as he was being tapped. I told him that he must have had a dream. Outwardly he accepted my explanation but I could tell it really didn't satisfy him.]

Entry #122 (Summer 1986)

I was just brushing my teeth in the bathroom and it smelled heavily of cigar smoke. Every time I smell it now I worry that something is going to happen. I turned off the light and went upstairs to bed. The toy St. Bernard was in the hall outside my door. It gives me the creeps. Anyway, as I walked into my room I glanced at it sitting there, and its head dropped over to one side. Then it flipped over onto its side. It's almost like someone whacked it in the head and knocked it over. I took it downstairs, put it into a garbage bag, and tomorrow it's getting thrown away. I don't need this kind of situation going on here. We have enough already.

Entry # 123 (Summer 1986)

Last week Aunt Nonie passed away. She was in the hospital when she died. Bob and I had gone to bed that night at about 10. I woke up sometime around midnight to the sound of utter confusion at the foot of the bed. There was mumbling and a bustling sound like people were all around the bed, between the windows. Then out of the din, a loud voice booming like through a megaphone. The voice was unrecognizable. I woke up Bob, but he didn't hear a thing. About 15 minutes later, I heard the phone ring. Mom came to the foot of the stairs and called us. She said that the hospital just called, and that Aunt Nonie had died. My first impression was that this bustling noise, and all the jabbering in hushed tones, must be what you hear as you lose consciousness and die. I got a chill from my head to my feet, and became very upset. Why would I hear something at that exact time that she died? Upon reflection, it sounded to me exactly like it would in a hospital when the staff would be rushing around a patient, trying to keep her alive. It was strange in so many ways.

Entry #124 (Fall 1986)

At 6:30 a.m. Michelle woke up to someone tapping on her window. She cautiously pulled up the shade and there stood Aunt Nonie. I know this sounds bizarre, but I guess in the scheme of things, it is just more of the same weird stuff that has been going on here for years. Anyway, she looked the same as she always did, except her glasses were old-fashioned, round. She had on a white top, navy blue pants, and brown shoes. She was carrying a white box tied with brown string. Michelle was aghast. Aunt Nonie said, "Open the door." Michelle started to run to the bedroom door, and a different voice came out of Aunt Nonie's mouth. It was a male voice. When Michelle got to the foot of the stairs, we could all smell really strong cigar smoke. Michelle will sleep in our room again tonight.

[I think that seeing someone dead outside of the window is bad enough, but it happened to be three stories above the ground. Why would someone who obviously loved the kids when she was alive want to scare them when she's dead?]

[Michelle's recollection of the event: I was really close to my Aunt Nonie. She was my grandmother's sister on my mom's side). She arrived with boxes of cookies and presents all the time. I was in my bedroom upstairs, woke up during the night, and heard a rapping sound on the window (always hear strange noises here, crashes, especially on the kitchen wall, and banging on other walls too). I got up and put the light on and listened carefully to see what it was and I realized it was at the window. When I pulled the shade up, my aunt was in the window! I knew it was her but the face was not her. Then it opened its mouth and there was a moan. I pulled the shade down and ran downstairs! It had her hair and body and she held boxes. It was specific to how she dressed. She wore a housecoat; those sleeveless dresses that snapped up the front—she was a large women. And she had Christmas presents wrapped in old-fashioned paper like from the 50s the wrapping paper was floral. I knew it was her, but why was she outside? Why on the second floor? That scared me. I was awake for a few minutes before I saw that. I think that was probably the scariest thing I ever saw. Luckily, it never happened again, just that one time. I have her mantle clock at my house that will go off on occasion if I think of her or if I am talking about her. I brought that clock to a clock person twice and they told me the chime was broken and there is no way it is going to chime. It has no movement in it, it is a broken clock. It still chimes randomly on occasion.]

Entry #125 (Winter 1986)

I was discussing Aunt Nonie's death with my mother while I was dusting the living room. I touched the lampshade, and the lamp clicked on. Later on, someone asked Michelle how she was doing. No one was there.

Entry #126 (Winter 1987)

Michelle went into our bedroom to call Charlene, and standing by our nightstand was an outlined figure. It was completely surrounded with neon blue dashes and sparks. The room didn't glow, and she reported that it caused no shadow. It looked like a "ball with a sheet over it," not like a person or anything. It was shorter than her, and was perfectly still. She stood there dumbfounded, just looking at it. She said that she couldn't move or say anything. The sparks dashed out in all directions and, as she stumbled backward, its main shape disappeared, but the neon dashes transferred to the door molding into two zigzag rows about two feet in length. Then they disappeared.

This is the first time that something of this nature has been seen. It seems to me that this thing was maybe surrounded by an aura of some sort. Not that the figure was seen as itself, but that the lights gave its shape away. It didn't seem to act in any way, it was just there. Tonight I am going to keep Michelle in here with us. I think that she is the one that this "it" is interested in. Bob agrees.

[Later we came to call this the Dash Man. You end up naming these things. Dashes weren't part of the thing, they were around the figure. Charlene was not happy with this house. Something was growling at her in the closet and she got upset about it.]

[I wondered why there was not much of anything written in 1987. Going back, I now see that our best friend, and my son's godfather, Dennis, got cancer around that time and he only lived through the end of '87—less than a year after he was diagnosed. It threw us all for a major upset. He was 40.]

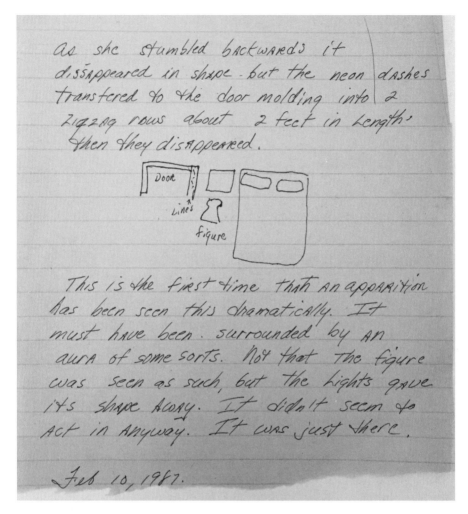

as she stumbled backwards it dissappeared in shape - but the neon dashes transfered to the door molding into 2 zigzag rows about 2 feet in length; then they disappeared.

This is the first time that an apparition has been seen this dramatically. It must have been. surrounded by an aura of some sorts. Not that the figure was seen as such, but the lights gave its shape away. It didn't seem to act in anyway. It was just there.

Feb 10, 1987.

Figure 4-1. *The actual diary entry for this encounter, which appears to possibly have been an alien encounter.*

Entry#127 (Summer 1988)

Dad has been having heart problems and needed to go to the hospital for tests. When we arrived back home, the whole house smelled like pipe or cigar smoke. It was really strong. As I said before, no one has smoked a pipe or cigar in this house for many years, and at this time we don't know anyone who does.

[I would love to know what goes on in this house when we aren't home. It's almost like "they" choose that time to make themselves at home and hang out around here.]

Entry #128 (Summer 1988)

Misplaced things? No, because the whiskbroom was hanging on its nail near the fireplace in the dining room. At least that's where it was a few minutes ago when I walked by it. Now it's around the corner on the other side of the den.

[This I don't mind. Possibly "they" will clean the house for me. What is it with all of this stupid stuff?

Entry #129 (Fall 1988)

I can't understand why I'm unable to sleep in our room. It's as if something wants to get me alone, and I always think twice before going to another room. I have heard the chanting and quiet conversations out in the hall many nights. Last night I got scared. That hasn't happened in a long time. The voices were discussing whatever it is they discuss among them, but it also sounded like furniture or something was being moved—dragged or scooted across the floor. That was bad enough, but the parting shot was when I heard something walking up the stairs, past my door, and up into the attic. What makes this so scary is that there are no permanent attic stairs—they are the pull down variety. There was none of the sounds always associated with the pulling down of the steps, just someone approaching them and, without missing a step, walking right up them as if there was a regular staircase there.

[Michelle is away from home and out in the world more than ever before. She hasn't specifically been pestered by "things" for a while and is happy about that. We still have the night prowlers, whisperers, chanters, and all other manner of visitors as usual, but none of that has been focused just on her. Sometimes it actually becomes boring around here. Not that I want more of it, but there are now so many little things that are repeated over and over.]

Entry #130 (Fall 1988)

Ah! A new scent is in the house. I went to bed at about 8:30 with a severe headache. The bedroom smelled like Lysol. It was all quite over-powering. I could almost explain this one although that entails a strange and complicated explanation. Aunt Nonie always used Lysol when she cleaned the house. She had two cats and we never smelled their litter box because she would disinfect it with Lysol. She added it to her laundry and did her general cleaning with it. We never used it here in our house, so there would be absolutely no reason to have that scent here. When she babysat the kids at her place, they would always return smelling like Lysol. It wasn't an unpleasant scent, just one that we always identified with her. Perhaps she and her trusty green were visiting us.

Entry #131 (Winter 1988)

Lysol, everywhere. The house is full of it again. Are we supposed to understand?

Entry # 132 (Winter 1988)

There seems to be increased activity around us today. At 11 o'clock this morning, Michelle went upstairs to get the vacuum for me. It was in the spare bedroom (top of stairs, left). The door to the room was closed. As she reached for the doorknob, the whole door began to shake, al-most knocking off the mirror that is attached to it on the outside. Then it opened and slammed shut loudly. She summoned up the courage to enter the room; she found everything was quiet inside. Later, at 3 o'clock, we slid a long nail through the latch to force the door closed. No one has been upstairs since, but I just walked by and the nail is gone, and the door is open. This seems silly to me since if it is a spirit, it certainly wouldn't need to open the door, it would just go through it.

Entry #133 (Spring 1989)

Michelle and Chris are going to the junior prom tonight. They looked so cute in their dress clothes. As they stood on the front porch getting their pictures taken, the broken clock on the mantle started chiming. It hasn't worked for years. Remember the expensive mantle decoration? That's the one. I think someone wanted to be there for this "family moment" and was letting us know—perhaps, even helping us celebrate.

Entry #134 (Fall 1989)

Michelle experienced a really strange one last night. She related it to me in detail. She had been asleep for some time when she was awakened by someone putting a hand on her forehead. She lay there looking around and didn't see anyone. All of a sudden the blankets began being tucked in around her by unseen hands. She was tucked in from her toes to her chest. Tuck, tuck, both sides all the way up and down. With that completed, there was a hand on her forehead again. She heard two women talking quietly by the side of her bed. "I don't know, Mildred." "The poor little thing is so sick." "Maybe she'll get better if we keep her tucked in and warm." Then, she again felt an unseen hand on her forehead. Michelle felt no reason to get scared. It seemed obvious that whoever these two women were they must have cared a lot for whomever it was they were tending to.

Entry #135 (Winter 1989)

There have been so many things going on around here. I sometimes forget to write them all down. Over the past couple of months, I have taken time to try and figure out what this is all about. No matter how I try to put these pieces together, they never seem to fit. We went from some really spectacular episodes to these smells of cigars. What is with the lights and the cigar smoke? In the first place, it is hard to comprehend that something like this occurs, and that it is like little signals or hints of something that maybe we should understand. But, how can we begin to figure it out if there are no specific directions? Maybe we aren't supposed to understand. Maybe that's the message—that there are some things we are not supposed to understand.

CHAPTER 5

DIARY ENTRIES FROM THE 1990S

"It isn't as terrifying to see something as it is to not
know where something is."
—DONNA RANDALL FILLIE

Entry #136 (Summer 1990)

Today, the alarm on our old clock went off. What makes that unusual, is that the clock has been broken for years. It simply doesn't work!
Such weird little things. "They" just can't give us peace. Just for once, I
would like to spend a whole month without "their" stupid goings on.

Entry #137 (Winter 1990)

Last night someone came down the bathroom stairs. The hall light
was on so that whoever or whatever it was could be seen. I thought it was
Michelle so I called out to her, but there was no answer. I sat up in bed and
saw an elongated figure standing by the wall. It was not in proportion to
the surrounding feature in the room. It was so bizarre that I just sat there
and looked at it. First, I made sure that I was awake, and I certainly was.
Anyway, it was very tall and also very thin. Its head almost touched the
ceiling! What was even stranger was that it was standing exactly where
the vanity is, which was hard to absorb, but there it stood, occupying the
very same space. My first rational reaction was it can't be there because
the vanity is there. I tried to make out a face, but it was just a dark solid-
looking shadow. It had a very long head, narrow shoulders, and a very long
body. I wasn't afraid because it just kind of stood there not moving.

Figure 5-1. *A view into the room with the vanity where the first close encounter happened.*

It appeared to have very long hair, at least down below the shoulders. Its arms were very long. It had a round area at the top, which appeared to be a head, but there were no facial features. They were all very tall and thin. When in groups of more than one, they move in a straight line. Then it just faded away. It was the first close encounter inside.

[These figures were the same as the ones we observed passing outside between the trees many years later. I don't know why I didn't get scared. At this point, I think that it's better to see what is here. It isn't as terrifying to see something as it is to not know where something is. I'm actually surprised at my reaction. Another thing, I've realized that whenever we change into a different bedroom, I make sure that Bob is between the door and me. I don't want to sleep near a door. I'm not afraid of what might come into the house, but what is already here.]

Entry #138 (Winter 1990)

Michelle and I have recently had many discussions regarding the unexplainable situations that have occurred here in this house through the years. It has seemed for a long time that the women of the house are the ones who bear the brunt of the attention from our visitors. There are periods during which it remains so quiet and calm around here that it seems normal, but then it always starts again. Neither one of us has any answers. In the end she always groans and says, "Why me?" I think the frustration of not understanding *why* "they" are here is the problem. It happens in spurts and spats, and most of the experiences are unrelated; there is no obvious pattern. I know the rings disappearing and the smells and the like are similar. What none of us understands is what it all means, and if it is even supposed to mean something. Maybe it is random. Maybe this is just the "meeting place" between their realm and ours.

Entry #139 (1990–1992)

[I have not written for a long while. Dad passed away after a lengthy stay in the hospital. We have had a rough time about it and I have not cared what "they" do.

Mom tried to sell the house, but had no luck due to its size and condition. Dad was sicker than we knew, and wasn't able to do a lot of things he wanted to. We bought another house in town and moved so that she could clear out the house. We lived for two years in a "clear" house. The kids are growing up fast, and Mom wants us to buy the house from her. She can live with us if we do buy it. Bob agrees that he'd like to have her there. It makes sense to all concerned.

We bought the house, but still haven't sold our other one. Mom, the lawyers, and the rest of us worked out a deal that is acceptable to everyone involved. We were able to afford it, although our first night back here, we lay in bed looking at each other. At the same time we both said, "We must be out of our minds!"]

Entry #140 (Fall 1992)

Tim has been around a lot lately and has also experienced some of the very strange things that occur here. This "condition," for lack of a better term, doesn't seem to care who it shares its presence with, as long as the person is accepted here, and is in the house.

Entry# 141 (Winter 1992)

Today we had a birthday party for Mom. We were cleaning up the house ahead of time. Michelle was in the kitchen, Bob was in the dining room, and I was in the den. I was passing by the cellar door on my way into the dining room and the door at the top of the cellar stairs started shaking violently, producing a good deal of noise. Everyone came running to where I was and we just stood there watching, without speaking. It was as if something had taken hold of the doorknob on the other side. The doorknob was twisting wildly. What a racket it made. What do you do in a situation like that? Do you open the door and see what it is that is responsible? I think not! It went on for about 30 seconds while we all stood there. We looked at each other expecting someone to make a move and open the door. It was immediately obvious that we all had the same idea—don't do it! Eventually, Tim got a rush of adrenalin. He yanked the door open and we all looked down the stairs. Nothing was there. There was no way anyone could have gotten into the cellar without us knowing about it.

Entry #142 (Winter 1992)

[This entry can be given a title. I will call it "The Terrified Entity." I was glad that this one happened, because it brought forth an entirely new possibility—theory—to me. I know there have been theories before, but this one makes some sense even though it goes against everything I have believed. I will explain after I relate this entry.]

Michelle and her boyfriend were lying on the living room floor watching television last night. Looking up into the staircase, they saw someone sitting on one of the steps, but ignored it, thinking it was Bob Jr. spying on them. They actually had a quiet discussion about his watching them. They couldn't see the whole being, but only a thin arm and elbow poking out toward the edge of the step. Tim called up the stairs that they saw him and he could quit spying on them; the figure didn't move. Tim got up and raced up the stairs toward what he thought was Bob. When he got to the spot where they had seen the arm, nothing was there. Directly in front of Tim, he heard unseen footsteps scrambling up the stairs in a frantic, thrashing manner. Tim continued after "it."

At the top of the staircase, "it" apparently slammed into Bob's bedroom door, made a sharp left, and continued through the closed door into the spare room. Bob, who was in his room, yanked his door open to see what all the noise was about, just as Tim ran passed. Together, they opened the door to the spare room, where they found the curtains were twisted halfway up the closed window, and still swaying.

[Well, now I have something else to consider. This experience certainly makes it seem like whatever it was on the stairs was more afraid of Tim than he was of it. With all of the theories I've come up with, none of them fit the situation here. Suppose that the two or three-dimensional theory was working here. Someone once explained it to me. Seems that there could be two or three different dimensions in the same spot. So, there could be different people doing different things in different time-frames, but in the same place. If this was true, and it could actually happen, then possibly someone was just minding their own business—in their own realm or time period—when Tim appeared, and that person saw Tim as the spirit, instead of vice-versa. Seems like a long shot, but why then would something run from him in such a panic?]

Entry #143 (Summer 1993)

Bob asked me this morning who was pounding on the headboard of the bed all night. It kept waking him up and he was really grouchy over it. I slept pretty well for a change and didn't hear anything. He said it sounded like someone hitting their chest with a clenched fist. I don't know about it because I hadn't heard it.

[This is the first time in a long while that he has mentioned that he heard something. He usually refuses to even discuss it with me. That's one reason that it was a good thing that everyone was there to see the exploding plate episode. (See diary entry #153 later in the chapter.)]

Entry #144 (Summer 1993)

Last night everyone was kept awake by a loud thumping noise coming from inside the walls. It seemed to be everywhere. Mom finally got up and started yelling at "it" and basically gave it hell for keeping everyone awake. I had to laugh. Here is an intelligent woman, standing in the

middle of a dark room, telling something that she can't see to shut up!
Well, it seemed to work because before long, it stopped.

Entry #145 (Summer 1993)

There are some really, really strange things happening that aren't related to the house. Is this some kind of a nightmare? I can't comprehend
how anyone would ever believe me if I told them all of this. How could I
explain it? I see no way to make anyone understand. I've heard of similar things happening elsewhere, but I believe most people would think
we are crazy. It's incredible to actually witness these things. Absolutely
incredible! Our minister understands and has explained his viewpoint
on the subject. It was with great reluctance that we shared our experiences with him, but we knew he wouldn't judge us badly because of the
situation. He has stated that because he believes that there is a spiritual
afterlife, that if someone was extremely close to us in life, or extremely
attached to the house in life, then they may want to remain here after
death. And, apparently, that would have to be an option. He didn't sense
any danger, and assured us that it was not a harmful presence. More than
likely, in fact, it was someone that we knew—someone who knew us. He
blessed the house and left. Of course he had no suggestions about what
we could do to make them go away.

Entry #146 (Fall 1993)

As is obvious, it didn't take long for Tim to experience some of the
"fun" we've all had around here. Michelle hasn't told him anything about
the house because she is concerned that he might think we're all crazy. He slept on the couch last night in the downstairs living room. This
morning, he related that "something" had lifted him off the couch about
six inches and held him there for several seconds, then very gently laid
him back down. Oddly, I thought, he didn't seem at all bothered by it and
acted genuinely interested in what caused the experience. Michelle told
him that he must have been dreaming, but he said "no," he was awake.
We found out later that the house he lives in has the same sort of occurrences as ours and that they also keep it a private matter. Good! Now we
have someone in our lives who understands.

Entry #147 (Spring 1994)

Oh, this is actually funny. Bob woke up this morning with his pillowcase tied around his pillow. It was pulled together in the middle and looked like a huge bow tie. These "things" are really humorous. He reported that during the night he had not been disturbed by it, never felt a thing. The look on his face when he discovered it was priceless.

Entry #148 (Winter 1994)

This morning when I was in the kitchen I heard scraping sounds coming from the living room. I thought it was Mom so I called out and asked her what she was doing. She didn't answer me. I heard it again, and called out again. She still didn't answer so I stepped into the room to look around. All of the furniture was pushed into the middle of the room in a haphazard fashion. My first thought was why she would do that. I called her again, and heard the upstairs toilet flushing and the door open into the upstairs hall. I called her again, and that time she answered. I asked her if she had been downstairs, and she said no, that she had been lying on the bed reading.

Entry #149 (Spring 1995)

Bob's friend Sarah is a regular visitor around here. They met in college and because she lives in New Milford, she has to travel back and forth a lot. We gave her a room to use so that she could take a break once in a while from the drive. She was raised in a religious family and doesn't believe in ghosts or anything of that nature. Sarah has the upstairs corner bedroom, and we respect it as her own private space. After many, many overnight stays, she has begun to relate information about our visitors to me. She looks unconvinced such things could have happened, even while she relates the experiences to me, and never gives a personal opinion as to the cause. I believe that as time passes, she will come to her own conclusions about it. She informed me that something had been following her around the house for several weeks. I asked her what she meant by "following." She related to me that whenever she walked, and wherever she walked, as her feet would hit the floor they were followed by the sound of another set of feet hitting the floor just behind her. She said that it was very distinctive and wasn't an echo. She said it even happened when she walked on the carpets. In another experience, she said she came home from school one day and approached her bedroom door. As she walked down the hall toward her room, she noticed daylight coming from under her door, which is normal. What wasn't normal, was that she saw the shadow of feet whisk across the floor. She knew no one was home, but didn't consider the fact that someone might have broken in and was in that room. She went on in, and only one thing seemed to have been disturbed—the statue of the fisherman was rocking back and forth. She had a fit, made me take it out of her room, and refused to even walk by it when it was within sight.

[The fisherman was a gift from Mom and Dad one year for Christmas. I had wanted one for a really long time. It's the kind that looks like a wood carving, that you see in fish markets.]

At this point in time, we are experiencing the old familiar stirrings. For so long, we have wondered why this house draws these types of happenings. I have been given a chance to add some evidence about the things that have so long aroused my curiosity.

Bob bought me a digital camera for Christmas. To learn how to use it I began taking pictures, mostly of the inside of our house. The familiar staircase, the living room, and the family members were the first subjects that I photographed. The camera takes the picture, then displays it on a small screen at the back of the camera for a few seconds so that it can be determined if the photo is one worth keeping. One day as I was taking photos, I noticed a white circle in a photo that I had just taken. It was of the staircase and the circle was just hanging there. I took another photo of the same area and no circle showed up. I thought that it might be a dust spot on the lens, or a reflection. The rest of the day, as I took additional photos, no more spots appeared. The next day I photographed the living room and when I checked the photo on the screen, there were dozens of those circles. They were of different sizes and brightness levels, from small bright spots to large pale ones. When Bob came home from work, I showed him the pictures and he thought that there may be a defect in the lens, and suggested that I take the camera and have it looked at. I am the kind of person who would just keep on using the camera without taking it in for repairs, hoping that it would clear up on its own. I cleaned the lens really well. The white circles kept appearing and I mentioned it to my neighbor. He was intrigued and decided to try his camera, taking pictures of the same places. When we examined his pictures, the same circles appeared. This certainly puzzled us; his camera had never performed in that way before. After he left, I took some more photos, and in one of them a circle was moving rapidly toward the right. It sort of looked like a slinky, blurred because of its motion. This proved to me that the spots were not on the lens, but something right there in the air. I couldn't see them, but the flash from a camera caught them. All along I had suspected that something was really there and not just a malfunction of my camera. I told Bob that I wondered if the circles had something to do with our "visitors," and he acted as if I must have gone crazy. I ignored him and took picture after picture. If I repeated a picture sequence in exactly the same spot, the circles would be there and then would not. That happened over and over again. If the circles were stationary and located on the lens, then they would be in the same spot all the time and also the same size and shape. After downloading the photos on to our computer, I set it on "slideshow" where one photo shows immediately after another, giving a continuous sequence of events. The circles varied from shot to shot; sometimes there would be many of them and sometimes there were none.

One night on television there was a program about haunted places and to my surprise they were talking about these floating circles that could either be seen by the eye, or photographed. This certainly drew my close attention and when a photo was shown, I recognized it immediately. They were the same circles that I had photographed in our house so many times. I went on to the internet and found some more information on the subject and was surprised to find many photos of these same objects. The articles stated that these were called "orbs," or "ghost globules." So, at long last the presence in our house finally had a name. After sharing this information with the family and showing the pictures as proof I began the task of convincing everyone that we should invite experts into our home to investigate the whole situation. Bob refused to let anyone in because I still think he believed that ignorance is bliss. The rest of the family had been waiting decades to finally settle this long and confusing saga. Against Bob's better judgment, we overruled him by sheer determination and decided to invite someone in who might be able to shed some more light on the basic information that we had. At just about that same time, Bob had been taking pictures of his own as he also wanted to become familiar with the camera. He handed the camera to me one night and mentioned that he needed to delete a photo because he made some sort of a mistake. The photo, according to him, was light struck and not intelligible. I stopped him before he could get rid of it and looked at the screen on the camera. He had taken a photo through the door to the dining room. It was late in the day, toward evening, and the only light that was on at the time was one in the den, which is past the dining room and around the corner. The photo left me speechless. In the photo was a clearly defined woman, most likely from the Victorian era. She was floating in the air about three feet off the floor with her head to the left and her feet to the right. She was lying down it seemed, and there appeared to be a dog lying in front of her. From out of that vision came light beams that crossed the threshold into the living room and played across the door. Behind the reclining woman, there appeared to be a line of faces repeated one after the other. Okay, I thought, let's make the call and find out once and for all what's going on here.

I remembered a number of similar things that had been presented at the lectures of Ed and Lorraine Warren. I wasn't sure that they worked on this kind of case, but I needed an answer. I decided to call and see what they may think. Lorraine answered the phone with such a sweet and pleasant voice that she immediately put me at ease. I explained what had been going on at our house and she turned me over to her husband, Ed. He listened to my story and asked me some questions about the house and the experiences. After a brief conversation, they became interested and asked if we would let them come to our house and see for themselves what was going on. I can't begin to tell you how relieved I was. I felt honored that I would be meeting the Warrens. They arrived and greeted us and we discussed the experiences with Ed, while Lorraine walked through the house to see if she could get a feel for what was visiting us so frequently. I must say that everyone in the household instantly became comfortable with the two of them. They are two of the nicest people we have met in a long time. We all liked them. Lorraine came back into the dining room and told us that there was a younger man in our kitchen who was just roaming around and wasn't quite sure why he was there. He had wanted to contact her, but she didn't feel that it was a good idea at the time. She really floored us when she returned from our bathroom and said that the room had been changed. Lorraine said that when she went into that room she felt like it had been altered in some way. She told us that there were two women in there. The reason that we were so surprised was that the room had originally been a bedroom where Aunt Nonie slept. Many years later, Bob changed it into a bathroom, and moved the door from the corner of the room to the middle of the wall. There was nothing left to suggest the room had once been a bedroom. When Lorraine was upstairs, she entered the room that Michelle used to have as a child. She said that someone who had been in that room had a serious breathing problem and that it was a man. I had heard that sound in the past, like someone was having trouble breathing. It was a series of gasping sounds. We concluded our interview with Ed, and waited for his opinion on the status of the house. We all waited nervously (knowing in our hearts that it was "haunted"), but waiting to hear what an expert would say. Ed said that he considered the house to be haunted, but Lorraine added quickly that they were all human spirits and nothing to fear. They were both surprised to hear that we weren't afraid, but we explained that the situation had existed for so long that the fear had worn off years before. We then took Ed and Lorraine upstairs to the computer and showed them a number of the photos we had taken around the house. They were impressed. Ed called the house "Ghost Central" because of the sheer number of entities that pass through it.

After the Warrens left, they arranged to follow up their visit by sending someone from their organization to do some digital recordings. The organization, which they had founded, is called New England Society for Psychic Research. Through that organization they investigate situations like ours and use the information to study related phenomena.

It would be very interesting, and probably enlightening, if we could actually hear intelligible voices. The recorders were taken room to room late into the night and the results were a bit nerve wracking. The sounds of a harpsichord were picked up in the upstairs bathroom. The house was extremely quiet at the time. No one was moving or making a sound.

Because of my acquaintance with the Warrens and the interesting work that they do, I have become even more interested in this type of phenomena. With the odd contents of the photographs that I've taken and the strange encounters that still take place here, I have to wonder if this will be just the beginning of our knowledge, or possibly the end of it.

I still often wake up at the same time as the house number and still check the time while driving in my car and it's usually the same. The clock in the store usually shows this time as does the clock on the church downtown when I happen to be passing and look at it. Is it a coincidence, or am I still supposed to keep searching for more answers? I have a feeling that I'll eventually have no choice. The answers will be there if they are supposed to be known.

[Author's note: The photos Donna mentions here have optical explanations that make them questionable and therefore have not been included in the book as evidence.]

[Donna's sister Diane relayed this story to me about the house number:

She told me that in the last month or so, that cash register sales receipts were totaling exactly identical to the house number and that it had happened at least five times. She said that it seemed completely crazy to her because she had worked there for around 10 years and could not remember a sequence like that. She said she even mentioned to at least three customers that it was my address. What was unusual was that with taxable items, sales, and combinations of products to total that specific amount, it would be virtually crazy to have that amount come up frequently. Then she was telling me how her friends are yelling at her for not eating right and how she needs to start cooking more and taking better care of herself. All of a sudden her computer turned on and startled her. It was really loud! Lol...it was a commercial to eat more fruit.]

Entry # 150 (Summer 1995)

Today, one of Bob's friends went in to use the bathroom while Bob waited in the backyard for her. I wasn't home at the time, but you can be sure she informed me when I came home of her incident. She was washing her hands and as she turned away from the sink, she caught sight of what she described as a "guy" appearing by the closet door and then walking around the corner of the door from the bathroom, going into the living room. He didn't come from anywhere in particular; he just appeared out of nowhere. She was agitated because she thought Bob had walked in on her. She quickly put down the towel and followed the "guy" around the corner, but there was no one there. At that point her irritation changed to fright—deep down, gut wrenching, fright. She hurried back outside and found Bob waiting patiently for her some distance from the house.

[I couldn't—I wasn't prepared to—explain it to her. The less said the better, I figured, so I joked that ooooohhh….someone was watching her, and booga booga, all that stuff. What else can you say to someone who wouldn't understand what is going on here? Nothing has ever hurt any of us, but if people were scared of this sort of thing, and they knew it was here, they wouldn't come back.]

Entry #151 (Fall 1995)

I went downstairs to get the dachshund. He's been with us a while now and he's wonderful. His one annoying habit is that he waits downstairs for us to go to bed, and won't come up. He makes us call and call, and then one of us always has to go down and get him. He plays hide and seek until we get frustrated and threaten to leave him there. If we turn off the light upstairs, he cries at the foot of the stairs until we go down to get him, and then the game starts all over. Well, I had the honor of getting him last night. I went into the dining room, picked him up, and turned off the light. I got this horrifying feeling. A split second later, something tapped me on the right shoulder. Needless to say, I made it up the stairs in record time.

Entry #152 (Winter 1995)

Tim and I were in the kitchen. I was at the sink with my back to the room, and Tim was at the counter to my right facing away from me. I was talking to him and he was bantering back to me as he fixed himself something to snack on.

All of a sudden he very quietly said, "Mom, look over there. Don't say anything, just look." I couldn't imagine what he wanted me to look at, but I did just as he had requested. We both stood and watched as a "spirit" slowly materialized by the closet door. Its head had already appeared, and then its body began to emerge. When fully visible, it appeared to be a young man, but his face was turned away in the direction in which he was moving. He was slowly headed toward the door into the living room. It was a fairly solid image, but the figure had no left leg. The dog was wandering through the kitchen at the time, and walked right through where his visible leg was. The figure remained visible for a number of seconds, while we just stood there and gaped at him. He didn't appear to realize we were there. What was extremely odd was that he was dressed in contemporary clothing. We could clearly see that he had on gray dress pants, a long-sleeve powder blue oxford shirt, and one black loafer. He appeared to have a short haircut, light sandy brown in color. He was so distinct that we could see a loop on the back of his shirt, just above the pleat. He started to disappear just as he went to his left, around the corner. Tim ran into the room while I cowered by the sink, He said, "Mom, you should feel it in here; it's like ice."

[Why would a spirit be dressed in a current style? I always thought that a spirit must be associated with the house or something in order to haunt it. I wracked my brains and couldn't think of one person living or dead who looked like that. Well, I don't know what to think at this point. Seems to get more and more confusing as time goes by. I have even stopped trying to second-guess this situation. It appears that there is no way to possibly figure out what is going on here. Things got weirder when around that same time, I was driving down the very familiar Klug Road and I saw a house that was never there before! It had lights on inside and everything. I didn't see any people. It looked welcoming and normal, sort of a 1970s type of house, maybe something like a raised ranch. Then a few days later, I made it a point to look again since I knew there never was a house there, and it was gone. I know that road and the house that was there next to this "phantom" house well. That really puzzled me.]

Entry #153 (Fall 1996)

We were just having dinner and my food was in the middle of my plate. I had served everyone else and had just pulled my chair up to the table. This is absolutely amazing, because my plate exploded. It didn't

Figure 5-2. *The area where the "phantom house" was seen. It was right where the trees are sparse.*

crack or split, but just plain exploded. There wasn't a piece left any bigger than a toothpick. My ziti didn't move one inch, but ended up flat on the table in one bunch without so much as disturbed sauce. Thank God, no one got cut by the flying glass. You should have seen the look on everyone's faces when it happened. It made such a loud noise that everyone ducked and jumped from where they were. No reason whatsoever for that to happen. The macaroni wasn't all that hot when the plate smashed. No one else's dish broke. I couldn't believe it! After we regained our composure, everyone started to laugh.

[When I said no bigger than a toothpick, I meant that literally! The pieces were really that small.]

Entry #154 (Winter 1996)

There was a long, creaking sound coming from the den. I checked but nothing was in there. It was almost like a wild goose chase because as soon as I got to the den, the creaking came from upstairs in the bedroom. I went to the bedroom, and the creaking moved up into the hall. I followed, and then it went down into the living room. Alright already! What is it, funny to you "guys"?

Entry # 155 (Spring 1998)

Last night a curious thing happened to me. I was reading and a voice said to me, "I am benevolent." I heard it as plain as day. What was so strange is that it was neither male nor female; it was just a voice. Now, I don't want to appear to be stupid, but I went to the dictionary and looked up the word. It means well-wishing, friendly, charitable.

[Suddenly, this puts a whole new slant on things. If it can be believed, that is. I don't know where the voice came from, but it gave me a sense of calm. I wonder if it is the entity who has been around here for so long. So, when we pass away to wherever, we become asexual. There are no men or women? It seems puzzling to me, but I suppose nobody knows for sure.]

Entry # 156 (Summer 1998)

I think I should take the opportunity again to try to put the pieces together. I know that this has been going on for many, many years. I wonder if this had gone on before we all moved here. I don't think that anything tragic happened here although I can't say for sure, because I don't know the whole history of this house. I do know that for whatever the reason, whoever leaves is always drawn back here. My parents married and moved away, then came back. My aunt moved away, and came back. My sister moved away, and came back. Bob and I moved away, and came back. That's strange in itself. But, different things that have happened are hard to put into any sort of order or meaningful context. We have the sightings of various "its." The elongated thing in the bathroom upstairs, the woman in the polka-dotted dress, the long haired "angel," the small thing that looked around our doorway one night, the man in the top hat and tails, the neon "dash man," Casper the ghost on the painting. What the heck? I can't figure the connection. Then, on top of all that is the cigar smell, and the missing and misplaced jewelry. Michelle knew who George was when there was no way she should have known that. I don't know if this will ever end. Will it just go on and on from one weird thing to another? Someday in the future will another family move in here and experience the same things? Will we be unable, or unwilling to move from here from generation to generation?

There are more questions than answers. I'm frustrated and my parents are frustrated. Bob doesn't care as long as nothing gets in his face. He tends to ignore it.

In 1998, when our first dog, Skippy, died, I saw him trot across the kitchen floor from the other room. I was in the den and had a clear line of vision to the kitchen and saw him walk right to left toward the back door.

Entry #157 (Summer 1999)

More and more, I'm starting to think that this is an earthbound spirit of some sort. I am nearly convinced that it is a relative. I don't like the feeling of surprise that comes with this problem we have. Everything will be quiet, and the last thing on our minds is a ghost. Then bang, it starts all over again. I've gotten this far in my writing, and I never explained my family. I suppose that it would be interesting for whoever reads this to know about us.

My grandfather George was an extremely kind and gentle man. He was adopted from an orphanage in Winsted, Connecticut, when he was about 14 years old. The family that took him was looking for help on their farm. At that time, it was common practice to do this. He went into the service at a very young age and was stationed in the Philippine Islands. There he served in the cavalry, and was involved in the takeover of the islands from the Morrow Indians. In later years, he owned his own dairy farm and was a milkman, giving much of it away to needy families during the Depression. He was an honored and respected member of the community. I always thought that he looked like Bing Crosby.

My grandmother Rhoda was also adopted. The story was a little more tragic than with my grandfather, but it had a happy ending. She was the illegitimate daughter of a young English girl. The girl had come from England to serve as a maid to a wealthy family in Connecticut. She fell in love with their son, but could not marry him because of her class. When she became pregnant, she was forced from their home to avoid a scandal. On her own, and very young with no source of income, she approached the home of an elderly couple. Begging them to take her baby, she told them that she would return as soon as she found employment. She never did return, and the old couple could not care for the child, so she was given to a family who would raise her. That family was the same one that took my grandfather in, and the rest is history.

My father was brought up on Long Island in fairly wealthy circumstances. He was a child of short dress pants and ponies. His father died when he was a child, but his mother raised him well. He had an excellent sense of humor, and rarely became angry. When we heard someone laughing, it was usually because of him. He enjoyed going hunting, although I don't think he ever killed anything. He was also was a dedicated fisherman. He belonged to the local volunteer fire department, and served as chief, deputy chief, and in other capacities through the years. He loved camping, but not when everything went smoothly. He always said that great vacations were soon forgotten; only the ones where things went wrong were memorable. We never knew when we might find a rubber snake in our sleeping bags. He was an honorable man. Dad had his moment in the sun when he rescued a boy who had fallen through the ice in the river behind where he worked. He made a lifeline and crawled out onto the ice, looping it around the boy and saving his life. It made the papers. He was one of a kind, and I see humor in almost everything because of him.

My mother is still with us. She is my best friend. We talk on the phone every day, and I always ask her to go cruising with Michelle and me. She is my partner in crime, and although she may not always agree with me, she sees my point of view.

My mother was raised on a farm, and had a good life there. She played in the fields, picked berries, and had a dog named Fluffy. While most kids shy away from their parents when they get older, my sister and I fight over who will get to keep her. For now my sister has won, but Bob and I had her for a few years with us. She tells everyone that she has a summer home and a winter home. She is a classic.

Bob, my husband, came from a large family, which consisted of six boys. His mother raised them by herself and did a very good job. Bob is a driven man. He certainly is more conservative than I am, but even so, still believes that we have some unearthly visitors.

He is methodical, and intense. He keeps me grounded, and I drive him crazy. It's a good balance. There are times when I laugh so hard that I could fall over. He just looks at me in a strange way accepting those moments, but never really understanding them. Once when we went camping he was standing by the fire while our son toasted a marshmallow. The thing caught on fire, so he whipped the stick back and forth trying to fan out the flames. The smoking marshmallow flew off the stick, charged directly at my husband's bare chest, and landed there in a gooey mess. Being so hot, it caused him to scream and grab it in his fingers. He threw it on to the ground, checked his chest, and then turned to walk away. As he did, his bare foot stepped squarely on the hot mess, and he promptly hopped on one foot while trying to scrape it off with his hand. In doing this, he lost his balance, hopped backward a couple of times, and fell directly into a lawn chair. The relieved look lasted only a split second, as the chair quickly collapsed and he ended up on the ground. I thought I would die laughing. It was like a choreographed dance number.

I am always amazed that the years have gone by so fast. We have certainly come a long way over the years. Diane and I always have a good time together. When we get together there is usually a lot of comedy involved. She and I get along really well and always have. We run different ways and have different interests, but are very much alike. We both have Dad's sense of humor, but I tend to get more carried away at times. Our family history draws us close, and we love to get together and re-tell some of the old stories.

The last two members of the family would be Michelle and Bob, our children. Michelle is a joy. Now an adult, she has been married for nine years to a wonderful guy who treats her like a queen. She has gotten a full dose of the humor that abounds in our family. Through high school, she was especially liked by her teachers and could get away with most anything. The machine shop was off limits to students who weren't in the classes there, but Michelle would take lunch every day to the students in shop. The teachers called her meals on heels, because they could hear her shoes clicking on the tile as she went down the hall. They never stopped her. She also took guitar lessons for three years, but finally gave up because she still couldn't play. We bought her a red flying V guitar with a brass whammy bar that looked very impressive. She carried it to school every day, and although no one ever heard her play it, they assumed that she could. The harpists and other members of the orchestra were outraged when she was awarded "Best Musician" of her class. She felt guilty, but accepted it with grace. She went through the crazy dress styles that were popular then, and her dad and I always get a kick out of how she's changed. She used to swear that heavy metal was the best, and our house would be rocking off the foundation as she blared her favorite music. Now very subdued, we can find her in her pansy garden, playing with her rescued dogs, or refinishing furniture in her spare time. We have always had a very close relationship, and to this day she can wrap us around her little finger. Michelle has had some unusual situations happen in her own house, which is an 1880s Victorian about twenty miles from us. I still think that she is the missing piece in the broad picture of what our "visitors" were interested in. I babysit her dogs when she and Tim travel, and have had some situations arise while I was there in that house. Once, while I was asleep in their room, I heard a crash at the foot of the stairs. The dogs were on the bed with me, and didn't bark. In the morning when I went downstairs, a ship made of seashells was lying on one of the stairs. It had previously been on the windowsill upstairs, about six feet from the edge of the stairs. It couldn't have just fallen and slid across the floor; it had to have taken a flying leap and jumped over the railing. Oddly, not even one shell broke. Another thing that happened, which was witnessed by ten people, occurred at a birthday party she held for me. She has an antique piano in her dining room, and the top is adorned with family pictures. There are large frames, small frames, square, and oval. Diane and I were talking about how Grandpa George used to take us for popsicles in the summer and would let us ride in the back of his truck. We were reliving memories about him. We sat down to eat, and because her dining room is fairly small, she placed her father and me at a single table, near the front of the piano. While we were eating, suddenly a picture on top of the piano lifted up, raised over two pictures in front of it, and dropped down onto the middle of our table. We all saw it, and things became very quiet. When we picked up the picture and looked at it, it was one of Grandpa and me sitting on the front porch on the swing. It had been taken when I was about ten years old.

Last, but certainly not least, is Bob. He has grown into a very proper young man. We attended his college graduation this past weekend where he received a degree in fine arts. (Michelle and I have the same degree from the same college. It is interesting how such things happen.) Anyway, Bob is tall and a handsome devil with bright baby blue eyes. No matter what he did in school, not that he did anything bad, his teachers all said that all he had to do was flash his eyes, and they melted. I think his girlfriend, Elaina, feels the same way. He works at a company that makes harps, dulcimers, and other wooden instruments. He has become a master wood worker, but doesn't want to make it his life work. Bob is more interested in becoming a millionaire and I believe he will. He and I love our heart-to-heart talks. Over the last few years he has become interested in religion and will discuss in length the history, the theories involved, and the scientific reasoning regarding it. We have shared many special moments. I always believed that kids need to have lots of time to just be kids and sometimes just waste a day instead of always having to answer to authority. So, one day when he was in junior high, I called the school to tell them that he would not be in. I woke him up and took him to an amusement park for the day. We went on the rides, played in the arcade, and ate junk food all day. It was our secret, and to this day no one is the wiser. The most precious memories are made in that way. I took him fishing, swimming, and to the movies with his friends. We made tents on the clotheslines. I bought a huge blow-up dinosaur and put it in his room. We always had fun and, looking back on our time together, he appreciates that. He and Michelle have a wonderful relationship. They are very close and love to get together and tell stories about what a befuddled mother I was when they pulled pranks on me. Their favorite is when they mixed all of my spices together. They put everything in the pepper shaker, including green Christmas sugar. Bob and I were entertaining that night and I made mashed potatoes. When I went to sprinkle pepper into them, the green sugar came out and made the potatoes green. You never saw two kids hide so fast. They still love to tell that one.

So, maybe we have a bit more enthusiasm for fun than a lot of folks, but we have nothing in our background that would invite "visitors." None of us are interested in the occult, or have committed any kind of atrocity against society. We are normal, family-loving individuals. Recently, I spoke to a friend about this book and how it came about. She was horrified, and told me that we were glorifying this sort of action by believing that it happened. Also, that such occurrences could not be from God, but had to be from Satan. I can't stress enough that each and every one of these entries happened exactly as stated. No one can possibly understand what has been happening here unless they have witnessed these occurrences for themselves. We have watched all of this transpiring for many years, and it is truly unbelievable, even to us—not that it has taken place but its nature. Is it from Satan? Then for what purpose? Is it from

God? Then for what purpose? After so many years of these experiences, we all agree that it is what it is. Perhaps there can be no explanation. There is a middle ground somewhere, and that is where we sit. There are many more years of entries to go, so I continue...

Entry #158 (Winter 1999)

I woke up at 3:19 a.m. really disoriented and feeling confused. Of course it was the middle of the night and all, but it was different than just feeling tired. It was like a sense of time, wrong time. It's hard to explain. Anyway, I heard a little girl's voice in the next room. It was very clear and precise. She sounded about five years old. She said, "Mommy, read me a story." Everything else was quiet except for her voice. I sat up in bed and waited to see if there would be more, but the rest of the night was quiet as far as I know.

Entry #159 (Winter 1999)

Once again I have realized the amazing number of entries that are related. I really think that if I were anyone else, I would have been gone from here after #2!

Postscript 1999...

Even now as I walked past the door in the kitchen, I smelled the scent of spring flowers. There are none in here just now as it is February. Judy, the new puppy, has an invisible playmate that she jumps at and watches for hours. Oh, and I won't forget the photo that I took yesterday of the dark hallway that clearly showed streams of light coming from absolutely nowhere. Finally, a set of muffled voices last night that visited on and on with each other. I finally put the pillow over my head and drifted off to sleep.

Because of the period of time involved and having no reason to believe that these experiences won't continue for many years, I have decided to conclude my entries in this diary for now.

Those of us who remain in this house, and those who visit this house will continue to witness the never-ending parade of ghostly visitors. As in the past, we continue to deal with each situation as it arises. I believe that I will still carry on with my journal until such time that Bob and I no longer own the house. I have accurately recorded the experiences and have unraveled as much of this mystery as I can for now, but am sure that in the future there will be more clues to follow.

Dad's wish had always been that the location of the house—as a "haunted place"—not be known. In earlier entries I stated that I couldn't understand his reasoning about that. As I've grown up and become more aware of the consequences of releasing this information, I have come to agree with him. It is difficult to relate this type of information to the public without divulging the location. I realize that telling a story such as this would certainly invite curiosity seekers and more than one local reporter. The publicity would not be appreciated by our neighbors, who like us are stubborn old New England Yankees. Still, we have our close friends who visit and are amused by the situation here. One of them has a difficult time breathing when she sits in our living room. She says that it feels like something is on her chest, and it's heavy. Possibly, sometime in the past, a person suffered with this disorder and in some way the experience is transferred to her. Who knows?

You may not be alone as you read this. You may explain away that cold spot in the hall, or that noise in the upstairs bedroom. You may ridicule those that come forward with this type of information, but do you really know for sure that such things don't—can't—exist? Could you be a witness to these activities and refuse to believe that it happened in front of your eyes? A haunting doesn't discriminate between believers and non-believers. They come to you if you believe or not. Tonight when you are tucked in your bed, safe and secure, remember that the paranormal doesn't recognize security systems or locked doors. They may come up through the floor or down from the attic. It doesn't even matter if there is someone occupying the same bed or room as you, they will come if they want to come.

Our ghostly visitors are here for the duration—they will, in all likelihood, remain long after the rest of us are long gone. In the meantime, we are also here for the duration. Possibly one day scientific proof will be available for those who doubt us. Until that day, we who have witnessed ghostly phenomena know the truth.

The disembodied voices in the middle of the night, the thumps and bumps, and ghostly presences will continue as they work to find their ways on into eternity, somewhere between here and heaven.

Chapter 6

"It" Follows Michelle

"Absence of evidence is not evidence of absence."
—Carl Sagan

Michelle's Personal Experiences

My house was built in 1890. It has served several functions since then. Among other things there are rumors about it once having been a funeral home. The historical society can't confirm that, but there is a historian in town that says it is true according to records that he has access to. Apparently, the house was originally built for workers who were employed at the piano factory down the road.

There were two tragic deaths at the house. A man was crushed by a piano when he was delivering it to the house in the early 1900s. The other occurred in the 1970s when a young man was working on his car in the driveway and it fell, crushing him. He wasn't killed immediately, but suffered there for several hours before someone found him. By then, it was too late.

I like antiques. I had found an ornamental boat in the house, which was clearly very old. It was a ship made out of shell or horn, a foot long and 15 inches tall. I cleaned it up and put it on the windowsill in the landing at the top of the stairs (short landing). Almost immediately I started having some issues in the house. Mainly, things would come off the wall that were so fragile they should have broken when they hit the floor, but instead of breaking, they would roll toward me and land at my feet. For example, the ship would repeatedly fly off the windowsill over the landing and land at the bottom of the stairs on a wooden floor. It was a full story below where it had been, but it would not break. It was actually close to falling apart in my hands when I put it on the landing the first time, so I cannot see how it wouldn't have broken after such a fall. That went on for years. I kept putting it back, partially just to see what would happen. I probably shouldn't have, but what was I going to do with it? I liked it there.

We had a get-together for Donna's birthday. I had a big piano with old pictures of the family arranged on it. One of them was a picture of my mom and my great grandmother in a tiny picture frame. It sat back behind the other pictures. While we were eating that day, that picture literally jumped up over the other pictures and smashed onto the floor. We all saw it happen. We were just enjoying the birthday cake and passing the time of day. There had been no talking about ghosts or anything to do with our relatives. When I first heard the noise, I thought it was the boat. It was, instead, the little picture frame smashed to bits on the floor. How do you explain that? We had all been seated; there had been no one walking around. I don't have a cat or other pet. We were at the table, and there were no kids running around.

The Fillie farmhouse phenomena

It always starts in the dining room in September, the fall. In September a new phenomenon began. There came a banging inside the wall downstairs, like someone was trying to get out. It was very loud, similar to a furnace exploding. Clearly, that would wake us up. There was, however, some variation in how it presented itself. Sometimes there would be a pattern of knocks—three followed by two. When we would go down to investigate it would stop. Once back upstairs, it started again, often so powerful it vibrated the interior dining room wall. At other times it would sound like someone with a ruler was smacking the counter. Still at other times it more resembled cracking, or banging, or even footsteps on occasion. Although it happened both during the day and night, most typically we would hear it right after we got into bed in the evening. It wasn't an every night occurrence but it happened at least six to eight times a month. It was most prevalent in October and November. It continued all the way through the fall until warm weather set in. Then it stopped. Donna's father was constantly calling the furnace people, but they could find nothing wrong and could offer no explanation for it. We have been hearing it so long that we know the patterns it follows. I just pull the corners of my pillow over my ears to sleep. [Donna mentioned that she did that too and sometimes, although rarely, still does.]

When I lived there we would ghost hunt since we had more time. At one point, Donna began using the tape recorder downstairs in the dining room at night. Everyone would be upstairs and we would close the doors off while it was recording. Months went by and we heard nothing but the regular noises. One day when we were all home together on the weekend, Donna came to the rest of us and said: "I need you to listen to this. I am not sure what it is." It had scared her (Donna) so I really didn't want to listen, but I did. If you have seen *Lord of the Rings* you will remember how Gollum talks—the evil part of him. That came to mind as I listened. The tape began with some of the normal noises we were more used to. At one place it sounded like someone was unrolling a roll of fabric—a series of soft thumps followed by the sounds of scissors cutting, intermixed was the sound of running water; very weird. It resembled a faucet being turned on and off. Then we heard a voice that said, "Lie down," as clear as day and scary as hell. It is difficult to describe—like a slimy, evil, spit-filled, angry voice. I could not believe what I was hearing. It scared me so bad that from that moment on I have not listened to any more of the tapes. Who is that voice addressing? What is its source? Although I only heard it once, it continues to haunt me.

The St. Bernard incident

Back when I was in grammar school, I found a huge St. Bernard stuffed animal for a dollar. It was a good four feet long with a rubber face and tongue. My room was on the far end of the hall upstairs. I dragged my new treasure up the stairs and put it in my room. The next day after I had gone to school, Donna found the St. Bernard lying in the hall with its head bent. She put it back in my room and shut the door. The next day, the same thing happened. It was in the hall when I came home from school. It was most certainly not I that took it out there. When I was at home it was always in my room on my bed. After about a week and a half of such antics, my mother became upset. She said if I didn't keep that dog in my room, someone was going to trip and fall down the stairs. We always found it right there in front of the stairs. I told her that I was not taking it out of my room. It still seemed somewhat humorous to me and I was joking with her and laughing about it. To her it had become no laughing matter. Her mood was all quite serious.

So, I continued to make sure it was in my room and made certain that I shut the door before I went to school. She continued to find it in the hallway at all hours of the day. Not long after that it started to "come out" when we were home, even when we were in bed in the middle of the night. We put a nail through the hasp latch in the door to my bedroom to keep the door shut. It still found its way out into the hallway. On one occasion we found it propped up way down against the wall at the end of the opposite hall. After we discovered it, it fell over on its own. It had always been found lying down before that. I made a point of keeping track of it so I knew for sure that no one touched it. Perhaps that was its regular routine—standing first and then falling over. I wondered if we had caught it in the first part of its routine before it lay down. We would go to the store and come back and it would be laying there in the hall. It got to the point that we would regularly check to make sure it was locked in that room before we left the house. It was heavy. It couldn't roll around. At one point we considered that Skippy, our little dog, might be to blame, but he was so small he would not have been able to budge it. Besides, he couldn't even get into the room because we had a nail through the latch. It caused so much turmoil that we finally bagged it up and got rid of it. It had begun moving everywhere throughout the house, not just upstairs and in the hall. At the end it seemed that every time we found it, it was further from my door. I didn't want to get rid of it. I loved that thing, but it became creepy.

Thanksgiving

(Michelle explains this occurrence in Donna's diary entry #152.)

Tim and I were in the kitchen. He was picking the skin off the turkey. At one point his voice became low—as if confidential. He told me to turn around slowly and to look at the spot he was pointing to. He said a man had just appeared there and was going around the corner. He was missing one leg, but stood fairly tall. He was dressed in contemporary clothing—a blue shirt with pleats, grey dress pants, and well-trimmed hair. The whole thing lasted only a few seconds, but I got a good look at him. To some extent he appeared transparent and yet had been clear enough that I could see details on him.

Reaction to the picture of the mirror

There she is in the mirror. I can see her very clearly. And that mirror is always clean. Those are not wiping marks.

"Oh my God—I see her hair with the type of braids she had, looks like grandma gray! I just got goose bumps."

(See the color insert for a picture of the sighting in the mirror.)

Tim's levitation

One Thanksgiving, Tim was watching TV alone in the living room, reclining on the chase lounge. From the kitchen I heard him gasp. It had been loud enough to hear clearly that far away. It had not been a scream or yell. He immediately came into the kitchen as white as a sheet. He said something had just lifted him off the chair. Tim is not one to talk like that; he had indicated his reluctance to believe in things like that and was not interested enough in it to even talk about it. By the look on his face I believed what he said about what had happened. He was clearly frightened. He couldn't explain it, which was at the base of his fear. Clearly, he had been wide awake through the experience. After that day he would not go into the living room alone and refused to talk about the incident.

Seeing Bob Jr.

One evening, Tim and I were sitting together in the living room watching TV. I heard sounds behind us and thought it was my brother. He seemed to delight in coming down the stairs and trying to sneak up and scare me. I turned around, ready to say "Stop it—we're watching this program." Nobody was behind us so I glanced up the stairs. There was the figure of a young man standing there. I yelled at him, "Bob, c'mon down. We're watching TV." Underneath the kind words I was really mad at him. He didn't respond so I turned to get a better, full-on view. To my surprise, it wasn't him. It was someone close to his build wearing a polo shirt and dress pants. He had a crew cut, like my brother. Other than that his clothes were different from anything Bob would wear. The part of the stairway on which he appeared was well lit. Suddenly, he was just gone. Tim had looked when I did. He had also called out, saying, "Bob, what are you doing?" I said, "That wasn't Bob." Later we determined that my brother was not in the house that evening.

As I thought about it, I understood it was the same figure I had seen sometime earlier in the dining room sitting at the table visiting with my mother. On that occasion I had looked into the room and saw him wearing the same clothes. That time I could see he was missing one leg as he stood and walked across the kitchen. When he was on the stairs I couldn't tell if he had legs or not. In the kitchen it was really clear. You could see one of his legs moving as he walked across the kitchen and then he was suddenly just gone.

That same night

I reported a UFO to MUFON (Mutual UFO Network). We were coming around the corner and we saw these lights and we wondered what they were. It was like a big, flat, black rectangle thing. The lights were like triangles underneath. It was to the left of the road where the Christmas tree farm is. All of a sudden it moved slow. It was summertime.

Fall 2012: phenomena follows Michelle to her home

I went to an estate sale. Dale always has to get something. We bought a matching set of two Scottish terrier stuffed animals. They were clearly old and about a foot long and 8 inches tall. I put them on his bed where I expected them to remain. This past summer, I found one of the dogs on the bed in the guest room. So I told Dale not to put the dogs on that bed and asked him to keep them in his room. Mostly, I just wanted to keep him out of there. He said, "I am not doing it, Mommy."

Eventually we determined that although the switch would sometimes happen when he was home it also happened when he was not at home. It was always just one of them, never both of them, and it was always the same one that got moved. (I suppose that also means that it was always the same one that didn't get moved.) As I put it back on the bed where it belonged, I would often have a word or two with the—whatever it was: "I know whoever this is thinks it's funny, but if you want to play with the toys, please play with them in here." The same thing continued to be repeated. It was not constant, but after a week or a month it would be back in the guestroom.

Sometimes, when there is no one else in the house, I hear footsteps upstairs in the hallway. They are often accompanied by young girl's happy voices: "Mommy, Mommy!" and laughter sounding very much like little girls having a good time.

Occasionally, I will hear Dale's electronic toys turn on and begin doing whatever they are designed to do. I often hear a rustling in his toy room, which is separate from his bedroom. When I check, there that dog will be on the bed. So we have those things going on.

I began seeing two dark figures just last week. They only appear upstairs—never downstairs. From the bathroom you can look down a long hallway. On one occasion I watched the tall black figure of a person wearing a coat come off the stairs and move right across the hall to Dale's toy room. It moved very slowly. I couldn't make out a face but there was a head. It was more a form like an old-fashioned silhouette— solid. The bottom of the coat flared out. I had previously seen what I believe is the same type of figure in my dining room downstairs, but it was see through—transparent—and shorter, with no coat. It was just a form. Both of them had the essence of a male I would say. I just don't understand why I am seeing such things now. I've seen the one upstairs twice and the one downstairs once.

Chapter 7

Ashwar: The Invisible (but Not Imaginary) Friend

"In Eastern culture, people see ghosts, people talk about ghosts...
it's just accepted. And in Western culture it's just not."
—Jessica Alba

Michelle and Dale's experiences 2009–2012

When Michelle's son, Dale, was still a preschooler, and was asked to talk about his family, he was pleased to do so. He would mention his dad, his mom, and then his sister, Ashwar.

What a nice family! Only one problem: Dale had no sister.

Dale often sat on the floor or outside on the grass under the special tree and offered his toys by placing them all around the trunk of the tree in a circle for her.

Looking back, Dale's parents understood that the seeds of that "relationship" had begun even before their son was a year and a half old. In fact, when he was still on his back in his crib and mostly attracted to his feet and toes, his attention would suddenly be drawn in its entirety to a spot some distance away and he would smile and kick and coo, his arms would quake, and his legs would kick—all positive signs that he was enjoying something no one else could see or identify. It fit well into the life-long encounters Michelle had experienced with the paranormal and reminded her of how the dogs had often seemed to be playfully engaged with some unseen entity.

By a year and a half, Dale might be playing contentedly on the floor in the living room when suddenly he would sit up straight and turn his head as if in response to someone calling to him or suddenly entering the room. He would smile as if eager for whatever interchange had taken place and mouth the conversational jabbering at which he was becoming so proficient. He would crawl closer and then sit and watch as if entranced.

Once real words began to open up his relationships with others, such occasions would be met with phrases appropriate for the sudden meeting of somebody special. Once he obtained his sea legs he would toddle off in the direction to which his attention had been drawn and spend time engaged in some sort of give and take with…something?

Figure 7-1. *Above the bathroom door off the living room is where Dale would look up and stay entranced by "Ashwar."*

As he grew a bit older, his parents would sometimes watch him as he stood at a window looking out on to the very large old tree that stood on the front lawn. He would point and turn his head to one side offering phrases such as "That's where Ashwar is." He would offer a series of nods to his side as if confirming whatever the exchange had been about. Once

Figure 7-2. *One of the first encounters with Ashwar was caught on home video.*

Figure 7-3. *Dale pointing to himself as he tries to explain to his grandmother about what he is witnessing.*

Figure 7-4. *Another still of Dale looking up.*

Figure 7-5. *Dale pointing up to where "it" is.*

engaged in those ways it was nearly impossible to distract him with conversation, toys, or even the promise of treats. The family never heard or saw anything.

By the time he reached five it had become a fact of life for him; he had a sister. Her name was Ashwar. It had to be one of those more or less universal imaginary friends that often populate a child's life, right? Wrong!

When Dale entered school he began talking about his sister, Ashwar, telling his friends and teacher all about her. His descriptions were so specific and believable that when Michelle went to a parent teacher conference, the teacher asked her about his delightful sister, Ashwar. The fact of her existence had gone unquestioned; Dale was a boy with a sister—a sister no one seemed to know about. It got to the point at which Michelle

Figure 7-6. *The tree where Ashwar appeared to Dale. Photo used by permission of Ray Szwec.*

became worried the school was going to call the authorities because of the "missing" sister. It appeared to Michelle that his teachers were, in fact, suspiciously puzzled by her assertion that there was *no* sister. How must it have looked? Either the family was hiding away a daughter, failing to acknowledge her, or Dale had serious mental problems.

Dale continued to interact with Ashwar. She would ask him to come to her, to talk, or play. Although by school age he understood other people could not see Ashwar, he continued his relationship and showed no indication of being afraid. Nor did he waver in his apparent belief that she did in fact exist, regardless of other's inability to see her.

On one occasion while the family was eating together, Dale mentioned that Ashwar was searching for her mother. It suggested a significant turn in the story. He pointed out the window and up into the tree outside the front of the house and said, "She is stuck here left to observe." No one else could see anything and the boy just let it drop.

As the story of the relationship matured, Dale began referring to her as his friend and the sister references dropped out. Sometimes he would stare across the lawn and down the driveway into the backyard saying that was where Ashwar's mommy was and that Ashwar continued to search for her.

The parents asked the other family members not to enter into conversations with Dale that were focused on Ashwar. They should try to change the subject. Although they cooperated, it proved to be a nearly impossible undertaking.

As Dale became more proficient with language the story moved on to another level. Ashwar lived in the big tree out front. He simplified her description to a girl in a blue dress who had been in an automobile accident and her mother had been killed. His interaction with her pretty much moved to the base of that tree, where he would jabber on and play for hours at a time with his toys, navigating the grass and roots and moving to the right or left as they would encounter a stone or fallen chuck of bark.

Michelle sometimes wondered if she should take him to a psychiatrist so he would have somebody to talk to about Ashwar and might receive some sort of treatment to alleviate the problem.

Then the story took on a serious turn. In December 2010, Michelle had to go out one evening and took Dale with her. They were having a light conversation about Christmas and his toys and he suddenly became very serious and started to confess about Ashwar. Michelle called Donna from her cell phone and was very upset. Dale began to talk to Michelle on the exact same road and in the same spot where Michelle had talked to Donna about a prior life more than 35 years ago. The words in quotes are words he has never used as far as they knew.

Dale told Michelle it was time to tell her about Ashwar. She was almost twelve years old. A "few years ago," she and her mother were driving a "silver two door" car on a "country road" when an animal "darted" out in front of them (he made a motion with his hand). Ashwar's mother "swerved" and hit a tree, "splitting the car in two." The fire "department" went to the "scene of the accident" and there was "gas" all over the road. Ashwar was hurt really bad and had "blood all over her face" and her "left" arm was broken. She "immediately" went up (and he made an upward gesture with his hands) and went into a tree. She watched. They had to "cut the top of the car off." Her mommy was "taken" to the hospital and she died about two "hours later." She had a dress on, too.

When Dale was in the dark and worried about getting back "home," Ashwar came to him and "took" him in her arms and told him he would be okay. She had little "tiny" wings on her sides and she carried him "home." And then he lived here. Was this a dream? An out-of-body experience? It was very disturbing indeed.

At night, Ashwar would come to him in a "dream" and want to play with him. He yelled "stop," not because he was afraid, but because he was sleepy. Sometimes her mommy would come too; she was wearing a dress, but she didn't have a face.

Michelle has mentioned repeatedly to Donna that Dale yells "Stop it!" during the night. Before this, both of them knew something was bothering him, but he never articulated what. These were his first serious detailed words on this subject.

In 2005, when Paul Eno came to the house, he took an extended video of that tree. The results were astounding!

"During the replay, we saw a serpent-like creature slithering down that tree—it scared me," Michelle said, clearly reliving that moment with some emotion. "It just *really* scared me—we didn't know what it was and had certainly never seen anything like it there before. We didn't ask Dale about it."

There came a time when Dale mentioned Ashwar only infrequently. The following summer Michele had occasion to ask Dale about Ashwar. Whereas before he had always been delighted to relate his times with her, he refused to discuss her. He attempted to ward off additional questions by saying she didn't come around anymore. It wasn't that she was made up, but rather that she didn't come around anymore. He didn't appear to be in any way upset about it. It was as if he didn't see her anymore, like a neighbor you find you don't spend time with like you once did. He never gave any indication that he missed her.

In 2010, Dale took his toy vacuum up the stairs to my bedroom. He wanted to pretend he was helping. He got to the top of the stairs and called me. He was frantic. I took a second to get up off the couch and he called again and wanted me to come upstairs right away. I got halfway up and he told me that something was over my bed going around and around it. I looked to see if the ceiling fan was on but it wasn't. I asked him what it was and he said that it was a "black thing." Dale made circular motions with his arm to show me how it was moving. He told me that Ashwar brought Gordon to meet him!

Michelle and Donna both explain that Dale is not the type of child to make things up. He is honest to a fault. He's very blunt and straightforward about things. He has always presented an age-appropriate imagination when playing, but he has no problem differentiating between what is real and what is made up. As has always been the case, he has friends and enjoys his time with them.

The true nature of Ashwar will forever remain a mystery, but "she" is one paranormal visitor the family will never forget.

[Dale never mentioned Gordon after that one time. I am not sure if he mentioned Ashwar after that. She just gradually faded away. It just became more and more infrequent and because we didn't dwell on it with him, we didn't realize the specific point in time he stopped talking about her after this. He now has no recollection of it or will not speak about it. It's tough to tell.]

Who or What Is Ashwar?

Dale looked out the window and told Paul Eno that Ashwar was in the tree outside the front door. It was pitch dark and very cold. Paul couldn't see anything there. Paul knew, however, that these entities do not necessarily appear to the naked eye. He filmed the tree area with a Vivitar DVR 510N in IR mode and caught a type of entity coming down near or from the tree while his son Ben sat on the front porch. The following stills from the video were the results of that filming.

Paul later found Greg Harold, who, back in 1974, was having trouble with vandals at his home in Florida. He set up a Kodak Analyst super eight surveillance camera to try to catch the culprit in the act. Instead, he started catching these entities—similar to the one Paul caught outside the Fillie farmhouse. They have large heads, two short arm tentacles of some sort, and one or sometimes two tentacles in the place of legs. Greg continued to film these creatures up until 1980. He believes these creatures exist around the world and are some sort of alien creatures. The following photo stills from Greg's many hours of video with a comparison to our photo stills of Ashwar. The similarity is intriguing. In addition, the movement matches. Could this be what Ashwar is? Not a little girl at all, but an entity of a very unusual kind?

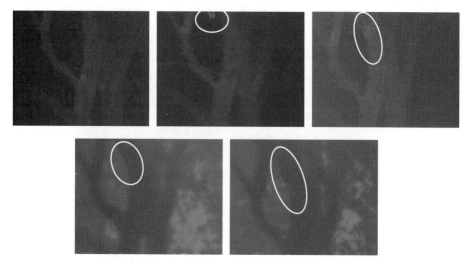

Figures 7-7 to 7-11. *These are stills from the video Paul Eno took after Dale looked out the window and told him Ashwar was in the tree at that very spot. Photo stills of video courtesy of Paul Eno.*

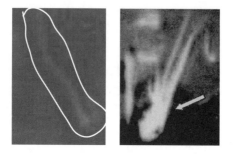

Figures 7-12 and 7-13. *Ashwar (left) and George Harold's discovery (right). Photo used courtesy of Gregory Harold. Ashwar still from video courtesy of Paul Eno.*

Greg has never felt any negativity from these entities at all during the years of filming and studying their behavior. He described them as follows:

- A head big for its "body."
- Big eyes.
- It seems to have a mouth.
- A short body about 12 inches long.

- Two 12-inch appendages; like arms but no hands.
- A long tail but in different views it looks like two tails instead of one.
- It looks like it floats around in some way.
- It can go through solid objects or structures.
- It can change its appearance (often changing into a "ghostly" see-through image).
- It exhibits intelligence. It first had what appeared to be one "suit" design and a helmet. Then, three years later, the suit looked different and the helmet moved up while the visor moved up and you could get a look at what was in there. The suit separates from the helmet when it opens.
- You can see the head and tail and there was always a little orb that comes along with it. It looks like it's about the size of a golf ball. Greg thinks the orb is the power source put out by these entities.
- There are no legs in the suit.

In 1979, one of these entities appeared on Greg's window. It looked like a little rodent of sorts. It was see-through, though. It was looking into the camera for a few minutes. Then this entity started growing—getting bigger and bigger—until it covered the whole window sill. It stayed there for a few minutes and then gradually disappeared into nothing.

This could be Ashwar. Of course, that is hardly an answer. The bigger question still remains: What exactly is Ashwar?

See the Bonus Features located in Appendix III to find access to the actual Ashwar video!

▲ Paul Eno captured a photo of a face in the lower right window of this home. There were no shades in that room.

◀ A close-up shot of the face in the window.

the HAUNTED
HOUSE
Diaries

This very intriguing photo appears to have captured a parallel world intersect with an alien in it? Either that, or it is a horrifying photographic error with an amazing illusion in it. With everything that goes on in the farmhouse, it might just be the paranormal caught on camera.

Donna, Bob, Michelle, and Diane all identified the faint figure in the mirror as "Minnie Gray" (the woman in the photo at right). She was Donna's maternal great-grandmother.

She took Donna's grandmother in after she was left on a doorstep and she also took Donna's grandfather from the Gilbert Home Orphanage in Winsted. Minnie told Donna's mother that she would gladly give up her life if it meant Donna would be okay. Upon finding out that Donna would live, Minnie sat down in her rocker and died.

▲ View of the farmhouse from Marc Dantonio's drone surveying the area. The red circle indicates a hollow spot in the yard where a haunted structure is likely buried. Inset: Dantonio, Bill Hall, and Ben Eno preparing the drone for flight.

▼ (left to right) William Hall, Shane Sirois, and Paul Eno live on *Behind the Paranormal* radio show discussing the investigation.

▲ This part of the basement, in the corner where the chairs are, held an undeniable energy. Paul and Ben Eno, along with William Hall, felt it on separate visits. William felt a force field—like energy and a feeling that there were many people there.

CHAPTER 8

DIARY ENTRIES FROM THE 2000s

"The activity level here is definitely increasing rapidly. We are not sure why it may be, but things are suddenly becoming physical."
—DONNA RANDALL FILLIE

Entry #160 (Summer 2001)

Tonight when I went to dry the dishes, some of the spoons were bent again.

Entry #161 (Summer 2001)

Last night it was really hot. I was lying in bed in the spare room, trying to sleep. Recently, I've been treated for insomnia (do you blame me?) and have been taking medication to help me sleep. I was trying to relax, waiting for glorious sleep to kick in, when I heard a voice coming from the corner of the room. It said, "Hurry!" Curiously, it sounded neither male nor female, just a voice. Right away I wondered why someone would say that. It was hushed, but distinctive. Hurry into sleep???

[Here is an interesting thought: Perhaps it was something that had been said years ago and had just hung there in the room, for some reason emerging at that moment. Now I guess I may be stretching it too far in my search for an explanation.]

Entry #162 (Fall 2001)

Tonight while I was in the upstairs hallway, the light in the living room clicked on by itself. I know it wasn't due to anything like the power, because it made an audible sound when it clicked on. I looked in, just to be sure, but no one was here but me. All of this stupid stuff, it's really aggravating, you know.

Entry #163 (Fall 2001)

Moms' shade seems to be doing some sort of dance. Up and down, up and down. Of course you know that no one had their hands on it at the time.

Entry #164 (April 2003)

Last night there were male voices downstairs in the den. I heard a very loud rolling noise that continued for several minutes. As I listened, I started to become unwound and went into the other bedroom where Bob was sleeping due to a bad cold. I still couldn't sleep so I went back to my bed and as soon as I laid my head down, the voices started again. I chastised myself for being scared after all of this time, and settled myself down on to the pillow determined to ignore "them" and go to sleep. Just after I closed my eyes, something pressed on my left shoulder. It was, as in the beginning, a pressure that was finger shaped. I relaxed immediately, recognizing that it was nothing more than a reassuring presence attempting to calm my fears, indicating, perhaps, "It's just me, Donna. Sleep well."

Entry #165 (Spring 2007)

Shortly after Michelle, Tim, and Dale moved back home, she came to the foot of the stairs in a panic and woke me up. She had been in the downstairs bathroom getting ready for work and was positive that someone had broken into the cellar. I got up and hurried downstairs following her into the bathroom. It was quiet when I walked in, but within a minute or two, I could hear very loud banging under the floor. There were sounds of large objects being dragged across the floor, and what sounded like multiple people throwing things around. We looked at each other with intense fear as we panicked. Just as abruptly as it started, it stopped all at once. We listened for a moment, and each of us went to one of the windows and looked down into the yard by the cellar door, expecting to see things outside or someone leaving the area. No one was there. The noise began again briefly but then just stopped. Michelle lowered her head carefully and quietly to near the heat vent, but could hear no voices—in fact, no sound at all. It was dead quiet. When we investigated the basement later, we found nothing out of place or disturbed in any way in the entire cellar. It is as if nothing ever happened there. Michelle and I knew that something of some sort did take place despite the lack of the usual evidence that such noise would leave behind.

Entry #166 (Fall 2008)

The activity level here in the house has increased significantly during the last two months. Last week, I put my grandson Dale, now 19 months, down for a nap. His crib was messed up, so I had cleaned out the toys, smoothed the sheets and blankets, and straightened out the bumper. After I left him, he was quiet for about half an hour and then I began hearing him talking and babbling on in an animated fashion. After another 20 minutes or so, I went upstairs to see what he was up to. His crib was full of toys and he was smiling and pointing up to the corner of the ceiling! He is not able to get out of his crib—he never has yet. And even if he got out, he would have been unable to lift several of the larger, heavier toys high enough to put them into the crib. The day after that, he began screaming when I put him in his room for a nap. He was terrified and clutched up at me when I reached down to get him. He has been waking up seven or eight times a night, sometimes talking and other times seeming to be terrified.

This is the same upstairs bedroom that Paul Eno noticed was strange. I believe he said that it was a difficult place to breathe. Last night, my grown daughter heard raspy breathing from that area, and she finally came to my room and climbed into bed, saying that she had seen a man in a black hat and clothes walking down the hall toward the spare room. She could hear his shoes on the wood floor—they sounded like men's dress shoes clicking against the hard floor. Anyway, I just wanted to write that things are progressing "normally" around here. She is moving the baby into another room.

Entry #167 (Winter 2008)

The activity level here is definitely increasing rapidly. We are not sure why it may be, but things are suddenly becoming physical. Not long ago, Michelle was standing in my kitchen alone. A clear water glass lifted out of the sink, moved up and over the edge of the counter and dropped, smashing on the floor. On another occasion in her own kitchen, she had put a large baking dish in her drainer, snapped it in to dry, and placed a few things on top, including plastic baby bottles. She turned away, and almost immediately heard a rattling noise behind her. When she turned back to see what it was, the bottles rolled off the top of the baking dish, which lifted straight up out of the drainer and moved across the room. It then fell as if being propelled with some force, smashing into a million pieces and breaking the tile where it hit.

Tonight we were talking and I remembered to tell her something that happened to me yesterday in the dining room. I had let Dale play in the large living room and just had the bottom section of the Dutch door closed between us for the minute or two until I was going to be with him. As I turned toward the door, I clearly observed a black object with sharp, pointy edges on the bottom right and top left. It was rounded on the top and blurry at the bottom, about the size of a bed pillow. It suddenly disappeared, and when I approached the door to peek inside and make sure the baby was alright, my legs began to feel like there was electricity flowing through them. Not goose bumps, but tingly, like a light current. This happened from my ankles to my hips. It went away after about 15 seconds. My daughter told me that was the exact sort of thing she had witnessed on three separate occasions. All three times, she saw that same "object" through the window of her front door. It looked like something repeatedly jumping up to get a look inside. When she drew a picture of what she was trying to describe, it freaked me out. It looked like the very same thing I had seen.

Her dogs, which have been together every day since they were born, have rarely disagreed with each other unless one has a bone. I have been complaining to her for the last month or so that throughout the day they growl loudly and constantly. I find myself going into her side of the house and getting after them several times a day.

I cleaned my small kitchen the other day and mopped the floor. The baby was having a nap at the time. The floor was empty. I turned around to wipe off the table, and when I turned back, there was a stuffed toy sitting in the middle of the floor. Her dogs were both sleeping in their beds.

Recently, the volume on the baby's radio is being repeatedly turned up. It is not a random occurrence. It happens at around 11:15 PM most nights.

While alone this morning, Michelle put a check on the counter that she had made out and was going to mail. When she went to pick it up, it was gone. She looked all over for it and gave up, only to later find it stuck between the doors of the desk by the front door. For years our family has stuck a folded piece of paper in there because the door does not usually stay shut without it. There is a latch, but it is loose.

I am wondering if there is something we should be collectively noticing or recording. This type of experience with things lifting up, sliding across tables and such is not in itself alarming because it has happened with some frequency in the past. But the force by which these things are being slammed down *is* alarming. Also, this black thing cannot be good. I asked Paul to advise us. I would appreciate any information or insight he could give.

Entry #168 (Summer 2009)

Last night at about 1:15, I was at my kitchen sink getting a drink of water when I looked out the window to the west. Directly over the top of the mountain, I saw two very large orange-yellow lights. I checked behind me to see if something was reflecting off the inside of the window and nothing was. I stood for a moment trying to figure out what I was seeing. There were several branches partially blocking my view and I wondered if, perhaps, it was just a single large object and the view was split by them. While I watched, the two objects merged into one. I then went outside on to my back porch, wondering if it might have been the moon moving down behind the mountain, but the lights were still there. I re-focused my eyes and squinted, looking away and then looking back. There was still one large object. Presently, it split into two again. Neither of the two lights moved, they just sat next to each other. The lights were bright in the center and hazy and more indistinct around their edges. Just a few moments later they moved in tandem down behind the mountain following an upside down "V" path, one moving down to the right and the other to the left. I would say that at arm's length, they each appeared to be about the size of a half dollar. They were close to the earth; certainly not as high as planets. They looked to be at about the height of a light plane flying over the top of the trees. There was no sound so far as I could determine. After they disappeared below the horizon I looked for the moon. It was shining with a white tinge. These objects were directly over the area in Goshen that we have been discussing. I have no way of knowing what they were, but I observed them for approximately two minutes before they dropped out of sight.

Entry #169 (Summer 2009)

Possibly, I should be questioning my sanity at this point. I was sitting on my front porch and again I saw a figure walking. This time I saw it to my right, along the wall moving from the road toward the rear of my house. I could see a human-like head and shoulders, moving at a fairly rapid pace. My grandson pointed. He saw it, too. I was sufficiently alarmed that it was a real person that I called out to it—the "Who's there?" thing. I hurried across the length of the porch to where it overlooks the yard, but no one was there. I could see the whole yard from that spot. Just as I looked down toward the cellar entrance, a milky white form in the shape of a comet moved into the wall and through it to the street by our main electrical connection. It left a transparent tail about two feet long.

Entry #170 (Summer 2009)

I was in the yard with my grandson this morning. We were facing the street. Out of the corner of my left eye, I saw something moving behind the row of trees along my driveway. Turning my head quickly, I was able to see the figure of a thin man walking toward the road. It appeared to be gray in color and was moving along at a relatively leisurely pace. He had thin legs and was swinging his similarly thin arms as he walked. He passed behind four small pine trees, and I could see him as he moved through the spaces between them. He got to the third space and just disappeared. The image I had been following just abruptly evaporated from view. His face was not visible or recognizable since he appeared more like a shadow than a being with discernible features. I was able to watch for about five seconds before he "left."

Entry #171 (Summer 2009)

One day last week Michelle came bursting through the door into my dining room. She was in tears and clearly terrified. Like me, she doesn't scare easily. She said that she had just heard a God-awful half-laugh, half-groan coming from her open staircase. It had not been upstairs and not on the stairs, but from inside the staircase. I calmed her down and we tried to look for other possibilities. Later on that night I was putting my grandson to bed. He kept looking toward the ceiling. He proceeded to clap his hands together and say something, which I could not understand. We clap our hands to call the dogs, but they were downstairs sleeping in the kitchen with the door closed. He repeatedly pointed to the ceiling and appeared to be interacting with someone who was talking to him. Whatever it was, it was maintaining his full attention. I have video of him pointing to the ceiling in his room, trying to show me something.

The house feels way too *full* again, sometimes to the point where it seems there is no air in here. It is physically hard to breathe.

Entry #172 (Summer 2009)

My daughter was sitting in her chair in the corner of the large staircase landing reading a Carousel book. She became amused at how her son, Dale, was tossing his toys out into the upstairs hall from his playroom. She could hear them as some rolled out and others landed with some force. She opened the door between her living room and my dining room (the Dutch door) and started to make a comment. She said, "God, he's making a huge mess up..." and then she stopped. He was playing on my dining room floor quietly with a truck and had not moved from that area for nearly a half hour. She said there was a lot of commotion and noise in the upper hall—clattering and rustling.

I will get batteries for my tape recorders tomorrow and put them out during the night to see if I can capture anything—a voice, perhaps. I have a collection of tapes that I need to sort through that contain the children repeating my words, a "God bless you" after I sneezed, and other cute things. I asked my daughter if I could put one in her room, but she said that she would rather not know if any such thing was roaming around that close to her. I will put one in my dining room and at the foot of my staircase.

Entry #173 (Summer 2009)

Last night at about 11:45, I followed a noise into the corner of my dining room. It seemed to move ahead of me and lingered by the Dutch door between my dining room and Michelle's living room. It can only be described as a strangled-sounding cackle. Everyone else was in bed and I stood quietly for a moment listening. I opened my front door to see if there might be an animal outside, but immediately determined that the noise was coming from inside the room. I pinpointed it to a spot about a foot above the floor in the corner. I listened as it continued for a good minute before it stopped. It is hard to describe other than a generic, unpleasant noise coming in an irregular pattern. After it stopped I opened the doors to check on Michelle's side of the house. They were all in bed and asleep with the dogs up on her bed. None of the dogs barked. I had not barked either! I have a new dachshund and he barks when someone is outside or comes to the door. He didn't rouse. This morning I asked Michelle if she heard it and she said that she hadn't. But, she told me that she had seen a black object move across her bathroom from the bathtub area through the doors where the washer and dryer are. She said it looked like a black bird with wings and was about the size of a small duck.

Entry #174 (Fall 2009)

Michelle was awakened in the middle of the night by a sound downstairs close to our adjoining Dutch door. It was loud and sounded to her like snorting or growling. She really didn't want to investigate, but wondered if it was one of her dogs. So, she went down the staircase and discovered that the noise was coming from my side of the Dutch door exactly where I had heard it before. She said it was intermittent and fairly loud. She opened her front door and put the light on to see if there was an animal outside. Again, it was clearly coming from inside, about a foot above the floor, on my side of the door. She opened the Dutch door (with great trepidation) and there was nothing there.

I have been seeing a light gray object in my den. It moves from right to left as I face the road. It is creamy in texture with darker spots, and stands about two feet high. It is narrow in the front and back—plumper in the center.

Bob found my long-missing eyeglasses and told me he had just set them on the nightstand in our bedroom. I went upstairs immediately to get them and they were not there. He said he found them on the floor beside the bed, even though I had vacuumed no more than an hour before, so I am certain they had not been there then. I checked the entire room and then the house and was unable to find them. This is an ongoing pattern around here. We have had jewelry and other items gone and then returned to their exact spot with much flair, over many years. They'll turn up again, probably in some completely different place.

Entry #175 (Fall 2009)

I was just talking on the phone while sitting on my front porch. I heard loud tapping on the glass in the door. At first I ignored it. Then I turned thinking it was my grandson, Dale, wanting to come out. The light was on in the dining room and no one was there. I kept watching and listening; it tapped three times, loudly. I got up and opened the door. My grandson was on the back porch with my husband measuring some wood. No one was inside the house. The tapping sound had been centered in an area that was about a foot off the floor. It was tapping really loudly, but even as I watched and listened, nothing was there to be seen.

Entry #176 (Fall 2009)

We have had an increase in things such as a black animal-shaped object leaping across the room. Sometimes it appears in mid-air, sometimes jumping down from something. Also, my grandson has been not sleeping well and informed his mother in his baby talk that "Unk Den" was in his room. He was insistent. It didn't upset us because he was most likely referring to our friend Dennis who passed away in 1987. He has picked him out of a photo before as somebody he knows but, of course, could never have known.

Entry #177 (Winter 2009)

We have had a flurry of experiences here over the last two days. Recently, I got awakened at 1:45 by a hacking, barking sound. It came from downstairs in my house, right below where our bed sits. I opened the window just to make sure that no one was outside and then went downstairs in the dark. I sat on the couch and listened, then went over to my daughter's door and listened again. Her section of the house was quiet. I went back upstairs to bed and was laying there. My dogs rushed to the foot of the bed and began barking. I made them quiet down and laid there for quite a while, not hearing any more noises. The dogs remained agitated but quiet.

Michelle was home last night and reports that she almost called us to come home from where we were at our son's house. She heard an extended and very loud moaning sound coming from the vent beside her stairs. It was not the furnace because it was not running. It was an actual moan, like from a person or what the old movies used to portray a ghost. She listened and music began to play through the vent. We have heard music playing down there before and identified the song as Mountain Laurel Time—it is always the same song. Then an odor filled the house like kerosene and it was strong enough to make her eyes water and irritate her throat. She thought something had maybe spilled or was going on in the cellar so she braved it and went down there. Everything was quiet.

Last night, after we got home, two of her old dogs got into a horrific fight with each other. The two of us could not separate them. They both received injuries. They have been growling for several days, and continue to bark non-stop. My dogs were barking all morning. They would run to the door, but no one was in the yard, or across the street, or on the porch. They were not barking in a friendly way. I must have gone to check nearly a dozen times. Then my gentle female Doxie bit me for no reason. She just tore into my hand. It's like insanity around here—noise, stress, dogs going ballistic.

This morning Bob opened the shade and aimed his remote car starter toward his car. He noticed that my daughter's car was not in the driveway behind his. It had been there when we came home at 8:30 last night and was in the yard all night. But, at 5:45 this morning the car was not there. Bob walked outside and looked all over the driveway and around the lower yard. It was absolutely NOT there. He came in and woke my daughter up to tell her that he thought someone had stolen her car. While he was waiting for her, he went back outside and the car was sitting exactly where it should have been. He came home tonight and told us in no uncertain terms that he was absolutely positively knows that the car had not been there. Fifteen minutes later, it was sitting where it had been the night before. My husband is a manufacturing engineer and has an analytical mind. Clearly, he couldn't believe what he had witnessed.

[Paul Eno's comments: On the car issue, I had a case in Massachusetts a few years back in which the car would be found facing in different directions in a matter of a few seconds when the family looked out the kitchen window.]

Entry #178 (Winter 2009)

Well, here's another one that recently came out of the blue. I was in the upstairs tub with the shower curtain closed. I heard the door, which goes from our bathroom to my daughter's bedrooms, rattling, producing a great deal of noise. I listened for a moment, then pulled back the shower curtain and looked at the door. It was vibrating violently. A dark spot appeared in the center of the door about the size of a golf ball. It sped out across the room and grew to about the size of a small tire. It took the shape of a propeller with three spinning blades. It had taken no more than a moment for it to appear, spread out, whip across the room, and disappear. It was grayish, almost silver, but I could see right through it. It was spinning so fast that it reminded me of a turning carriage wheel at the point where it looks like it is going backward. I looked up signs, and it closely resembled a radiation sign—those three, pie-shaped wedges with rounded tops.

Earlier, my black dog was walking from our dining room area into our living room and he was looking back over his right shoulder at the wall. He had his tail between his legs and he hurried along, all of a sudden scuffing his back end up under him as he went. He was so intent that he walked into the couch.

Entry #179 (Winter 2009)

We had an experience here last night that is sending my daughter and grandson into our living room tonight to sleep. She woke up at 2:15 to the sound of "clomping" up and down the hall outside her room. She had the door open but couldn't see very well without her contact lenses. It proceeded to make snorting noises, but her dogs did not wake up or move. They were on her bed. She went to the door and looked up and down the hall, but nothing was there. She went back to bed. The clomping continued so she eventually got up and took her son out of his bed and put him in bed with her. She closed her door. The snorting sound went to the bottom of her door from the outside, and she said it sounded like something was sniffing under the door. It scared her and she said the noise continued until it began to get light outside. Today she said it sounded like someone was riding a horse up and down the hallway. We are using the aero bed on our den floor tonight for her and Daley.

[Paul Eno's comments: Thanks for the update—all very interesting, especially in the context of other cases. Certainly sounds like a horse! I get constant impressions of an 18th- or early-19th-century horse and rider around your place, though usually not inside!]

Entry #180 (Winter 2009)

My daughter saw the jumping thing again near the door. That time it was smaller, only about a foot high. We have had the "corner-of-the-eye things" flitting about, and our cellar has been smelling odd for some reason. Last night we were not home. Our grandson went upstairs into our bedroom in the dark. My daughter sat here on the computer calling for him to come back down. He started to scream hysterically, then he stopped all of a sudden and said something to the effect of, "Bye, bye. See you later, okay," and then came back down the stairs.

Entry #181 (Winter 2009)

Last night we had an experience that was seen or at least heard by four people. My daughter had put a large toy train on the tracks around the bottom of her Christmas tree. The train is a remote-controlled "G" scale train called the Coastal Express. It required several batteries to operate, but some of them were missing. She decided to set it up there because it belongs to the grandson and she thought it would look cute. She was in her kitchen taking care of her dogs with the baby gate closing them all inside. My son was sitting on the couch with me, my daughter-in-law was on the loveseat, and my grandson was in the middle of the floor watching a Mickey Mouse cartoon on TV. We were laughing and talking together about the arrival of my son's new baby, which will be born in April.

In plain view of all of us, one of the train cars lifted up off the track, rolled over in midair, and flew across the floor hitting the wall with some force. I don't know if that's a bad thing or a good thing, but we saw it happen and everyone jumped. After we put it back under the tree, my son said, "Now that's just plain creepy."

Entry #182 (Winter 2010)

There has been something on my bed, which I noticed four separate times. At first it appears to look like a cat, but then it seems to turn liquid and just drops and is gone. Once, there was an indentation on the blanket in an uneven circle. The thing I am seeing is dark gray and the reason it caught my eye is that it seems to be moving, but when I look it just drops flat and is gone. Twice I have seen a dark line going across the room about one foot off the floor, which then shortens as it moves into the wall. My black dachshund seems to be very attentive to something and it has gotten to the point of being disturbing to Bob and I. He becomes obsessive about one spot in the room or another and watches intently, even getting to the point of trying to move things like tables and chairs to follow whatever it is that he sees. One evening he spent two and a half hours staring at one spot and could not be moved.

Entry #183 (Winter 2011)

I was woken up the other morning by a very distinct female voice, which was coming from the ceiling by the foot of my bed. Her voice was high pitched and she had a very sharp tongue. All I could figure out were the words "Because I said so! Don't listen to them—they don't know."

The night before that, my daughter caught sight of a very heavy woman slowly walking away from her bedroom and down the hall. She was a shadow and not see-through. The woman had a side-to-side gait, almost like a waddle. The woman went around the corner and into Dale's toy room.

When I was sleeping on the downstairs floor with Judy [her dog] on Monday night, I heard very distinct cracks in the basement under my head. It sounded like cracking a stick against rock. It did it about six or seven times and then it stopped.

Entry #184 (Winter 2011)

We have, for some reason, been getting increased activity and I think it may be something earthly from the past, present, or future. My son-in-law and Michelle were woken up this morning by a woman singing off-key in Dale's room. She got up to check it out. There was no one there but the singing carried on. It was loud enough that it woke up Dale too! The voice was familiar to Michelle, but she couldn't place who it was. The song was about Jesus and an angel but she was not familiar with it. Maybe it's a hymn? There was no music—just the singing.

This morning I woke up at 3 a.m. to Dale's large truck making noise in my downstairs den. It was racing and roaring. Bob got up and was puzzled as to how it could have turned on because there is a hard-to-reach switch behind the wheel. He tried to make it go on several times over the course of the day without turning the switch but he couldn't make it turn on.

There has been banging throughout the house with no apparent source. Michelle and my son-in-law thought the roof collapsed the other night and checked outside the next morning for sliding snow but it was all intact. We had not heard a thing during the night even though we are only a door away.

[To Paul Eno] I have to ask you if stress will bring on this type of activity. I had heard it does and we have been trying very hard to keep the level low, but things just keep happening beyond our control. We are all exhausted for some reason and have no physical energy to do much of anything. I plan on using the sage yet again and see if it tones down.

Entry #185 (Winter 2011)

While eating lunch at McDonalds today with Dale, the following conversation took place between us:

"Grandma, somebody was shaking my bed this morning really hard."

"Who was it, Dale?"

"Nobody. Nobody was there, but they were shaking my bed."

"It was nobody? It had to be somebody."

"Nope, nobody, but they were shaking the top and bottom really hard. It woke me up and they just kept shaking it hard."

"Did anybody touch you, or was it just the bed?"

"Just the bed."

"They shook it, and shook it, and shook it."

Dale came into our bed in the middle of the night saying the "moon" was bothering him again.

Entry #186 (Spring 2012)

I was standing on the front porch, not really near the edge, and I watched as my son and his wife drove in for a visit. I turned around and yelled out to my husband that they were here. I do not remember falling or stepping to the edge of the porch. The next thing I knew, I was laying on the ground on my right side. I had literally traveled approx. six to eight feet from my previous location on the porch. I do not remember moving at all, did not feel any previous oddities. Was not dizzy, was not sick, and was feeling perfectly fine. When I landed on the stone walkway, my feet were just below the third stone down toward the road from the porch, not counting the very large curved stepping stone up against the porch. I immediately knew I had broken my right foot and the emergency department at the hospital confirmed I had broken multiple bones, including what they called the ballerina bone that runs the outside length of my right foot.

Entry #187 (Fall 2012)

I saw movement going from right to left. They were visible, light gray, and see through. They were not walking but gliding. They were very thin and tall with what appeared to be robes and their heads seemed to be tilted down. They passed behind the trees in a row, and when they came to the last group of trees, they went behind and never came back out.

Entry #188 (Winter 2012)

Last night Michelle was downstairs in the living room reading by the staircase. Dale had gone to bed. She heard the chair move across the floor in the upstairs hallway. Thinking it was Dale, she called up for him to get back into bed. He didn't answer and things grew quiet. A few moments later she heard heavy footsteps moving down the hall. She looked up and saw a person leaning over the railing, looking down at her. She said it was completely smooth and gray. The head offered the shape of a face but no features or hair. The figure had long arms and fingers, which were clearly visible. It appeared to have something hanging from its arms, shoulders, and fingers—gray rags, perhaps. No mouth, nose, or cheekbones were evident, at least from that distance. Its bearing suggested it was watching her, but having no eyes that could really not be determined. Upon reflection she believes the rags resembled those on a mummy—the loose ends dangling. She hurried into her bathroom, scared. Soon after, she went to bed, but left all the upstairs lights on.

She is moving Dale back into his old room this weekend. Recently he has been talking again about the "moon" coming up out of his floor and bothering him. We are wondering if it may be related to orbs. Anyway, I don't know how much better the new room will be because it is the room where Michelle experienced all the incidents while she was growing up. To be honest, I think that regardless of where he is located, if something is set on bothering him, it will.

Earlier, I had been sitting on the edge of my bed when a dark gray block, a 4 inch by 1 inch rectangle, came right out of the wall. It moved down toward the floor, came back up, went back down, and came back up a final time before moving through the opposite wall. It moved rapidly in a zigzag pattern.

My dogs keep running to the front door and barking, clearly upset, but no one is there, not even out on the road.

Entry #189 (Summer 2012)

I was sitting at my computer and heard this sound to my right. I glanced over to see what it was and this dark, wedge-shaped thing came whipping across the room straight at me. The wedge made a slight squeal, almost like a car slamming on its brakes. It was not loud or long and drawn out, but like a quick second noise. It was going so fast that I couldn't keep my eyes on it. Almost what I would call supersonic speed. It flashed between my face and my screen and then was gone. Almost looked like a mechanical bird or one of those tightly folded paper ones. Shortly after that, my eyes were drawn back to the same area and something the same size and color whizzed up from the floor at the same size and speed and disappeared. I sat back for a minute or two and looked around but didn't see anything, no bugs, moths, flies…. It was dead quiet. About 30 seconds later, when I had resumed typing, something silently flew past my head, catching my hair, and seemed to go rapidly up over the top of my head and then back across the room.

About 10 minutes later, I went into my kitchen to get a glass of water and stood facing the window over the sink. In the reflection of the window I clearly saw something step out from behind the side of my refrigerator. It was blobbish and flesh colored. Had a spot that looked like a big flesh-colored head with bulbs of skin hanging off, arms were the same. I can only describe it as dark, but it was solid.

It then just stepped back. I immediately turned and looked but there was nothing there. I have no idea what this is!

[It was very manufactured looking, like a mechanical bird or tightly folded paper/origami. The big thing was just completely weird. It was flesh colored and completely lumpy. It's head was very large and had no features that I could see reflected. It didn't give me the feeling of being scared, but I almost felt sorry for it. Really fleshy, and it sounds gross, but like it had big flesh-colored tumors on it. The head was barely smaller than its body, which was very round and it didn't appear to have a neck. It looked to me like it had a right arm slightly raised away from its body and I didn't notice any fingers. More like one large round unit with what may have been a thumb. I measured the approximate size of it since it appeared next to my refrigerator. It was just about five feet tall.]

Entry #190 (Summer 2012)

Today, it was so odd. I was waiting for my doctor to pick up her phone and was on hold listening to music. I grabbed a pen and could not find paper so I grabbed a white coffee filter and put it on the counter. She answered the phone and I didn't need to write anything down. Later on when I went back to clean up the kitchen I found that I had drawn a house and inside I wrote the word "Hide." I swear, I don't remember writing anything at all and am puzzled why I would write that anyway.

Entry #191 (Summer 2012)

At the risk of sounding crazy, let me recount the time I broke my foot. I was, for no conceivable reason, thrown off the porch. I was standing there perfectly fine. It was a beautiful spring day. Suddenly I found myself halfway down the front steps laying on my side. My foot was in terrible shape—it was broken. There is no way that I could have stepped or off or fallen off and landed there in that position. A year later I found myself thinking about the incident. I was waving to my son and daughter-in-law as they came up the driveway to visit.

[See images on page 147.]

Entry #192 (Winter 2013)

We have been busy in the house and helping our daughter-in-law with the baby. Our son is working double shifts at the nursing home and in school for nursing. Busy, busy!

Yesterday morning when I woke up my quilt was kind of bunched up by my face. I looked over it and saw something moving on the bottom left-hand side of the bed. It appeared to be the top of two animal-shaped black ears or horns. They were very dark and pointed and separated by a space that would be head sized. I could see that they were fairly long, at least five inches or more and wider at the bottom. I sat up quick and they were gone. The tips of them were probably about four feet off the floor. They were pretty solid in the center but hazy around the edges.

Figure 8-1. *This is the walkway Donna refers to in Entry #191.*

Figure 8-2. *Donna found herself toward the bottom step in this photo! It was too far for her to even jump there.*

Entry #193 (Summer 2014)

Activity around here has changed. I saw some sort of energy that looks like when you can see the heat on a road. It was clear and kind of wavering. It seemed to come in shapes such as arcs and squares. I saw four or five shaped like rainbows coming up from the ground behind the house this week.

Entry #194 (Summer 2014)

At least six people I know have developed unexplained muscle cramping in their legs, feet, and hands. There is also a massive uptick in migraines for people in the area who have no history of them. I'm thinking it may be some sort of energy affecting people?

I have had involuntary leg stretching and then the muscles twist. I could hardly walk for three days last week. Our local town chatter site has others complaining of the same thing.

Entry #195 (Winter 2014)

Bob called me when I was in the kitchen making coffee. He looked down to see one of the ornaments rolling across the floor toward him. He was in the recliner watching TV. It rolled all the way across the room on the rug. And it was one of those light Styrofoam ones.

Entry #196 (Winter 2014)

Bob was sitting in the recliner with the two dogs on his lap and I was in the kitchen. He calls in, "Hey, the lantern is swinging again." I went in and it was just swinging back and forth, back and forth.

That lantern came from when my grandfather was taken in from the orphanage and worked on his first farm. It traveled with him up on to the property by UCONN and then down here.

[I slept in the living room the last two nights because my fat dog was sick and I couldn't keep carrying him up and down the stairs. I don't like sleeping in there, but when you think about it, what's the difference in this house anyway? Like nothing can go from room to room.

Still frustrated with this house after all these years. I just shook my head when I saw that lantern swinging. I thought, here we go again, what is *that* supposed to mean? We had everyone here at Christmas, all the family, and not one peep from our invisible residents.]

Entry #197 (Winter 2014)

I had a very swift and distinct visit from someone last night right after I climbed into bed. On my left hand side, I heard a man's voice. His exact words were, "Look out the window and you will see that you're free. My name is Leo."

It wasn't cold, no sound, no breeze, no nothing. Just that statement.

Two nights ago I had what looked like blue gas jets above the shower curtain toward the ceiling. They were about three or four inches high. They flared up and then died down.

Entry #198 (Winter 2015)

Interesting situation tonight. Dale was in the bathtub, Charlie was outside, Bob was in the den, and I was in the kitchen. I heard Shimmer growling in the living room. I looked in to see her crouched down facing the inside corner of the staircase. Her hair was standing on end and her teeth were showing. I thought that Dale may have gotten out of the tub and was teasing her, so I yelled in for him to stop. He was still in the tub. I stepped in and looked to where she was growling toward and nothing was there. She had a small biscuit in front of her and was guarding it from someone or something.

She is the first one to react to something like this since Skippy. She is protective of her belongings but will not growl, show her teeth, or crouch unless someone was to approach and tell her they were going to take it. She may react like that if Charlie was to try to get her food but he was outside in the pen.

Entry #199 (Winter 2015)

I was sitting in the recliner, the one that is in the corner near the staircase. I saw something fluttering above my head and to the left over the lampshade. I looked up and watched. It appeared to be a luminous, cloudy, white butterfly fluttering toward the center of the room. I can clearly see two wings. It was very definite, but there was no body. It didn't seem to be gliding; it appeared to be fluttering. The wings were cloudy, white but defined, shaped like a butterfly. It went up toward the ceiling and disappeared as it went right through!

Entry #200 (Winter 2015)

I had an experience tonight. I went into the bathroom and the wall vanity popped open wide—all by itself! My brown plastic powder make-up compact literally flew off the shelf over the top of the sink and vanity and landed on the floor. That vanity door doesn't open easily either. The makeup compact had some force behind it as it took off and flew. I also put my tape recorder in the living room last night and captured what sounded like a cupboard shutting and one string on my dulcimer being plucked.

Entry #201 (Winter 2015)

I grabbed my tablet and got a video of the lantern swinging by itself as it sometimes does. Bob called me into the room to show me. He was in the recliner under a blanket with the dogs on his lap and I was in the dining room complaining about having cabin fever. He yelled out, and I thought he said, "There you go ranting again" but he actually said, "There goes the lantern again." LOL

[Donna caught the lantern swinging on video. See the bonus page to witness it for yourself. Note that this could have easily been faked (although it was not). Therefore, it is not offered as "evidence." It is offered as a view at a paranormal happening for those who believe our story. I can tell you that no one writes a 50-year diary on different odd papers in anticipation of faking something. Therefore, the video is of interest to me and should be for you too.]

PART II

PHENOMENA IN THE FLAP

Although in the past it has been theorized that a "paranormal flap" is different than a haunting, we now believe that the proxy to all paranormal events is relatively the same energy source or portal, for lack of a better word, to describe this elusive parallel world intersect of sorts. Rather than there being clear distinctions that UFO flaps are over large areas and hauntings are contained to one house, we now know that the paranormal is much more interconnected. The silo approach to categorizing and looking at phenomena in its own neat category is no longer a viable working model. We must look at this from a much different perspective and see the broader implications. Quantum psychics is now providing the means for us to access better theories around how this all works. Science has come a long way in developing this; however, there is still a lot of work to be done.

The Litchfield paranormal flap is the poster child and proving ground to demonstrate that all kinds of phenomena can converge in one area—and over a large area—regardless of the nature of the phenomena. It could be cryptids, UFOs, glimpses into the multiverse with time slips, haunted houses (like the Fillie house), and roads with entities (human and non-human, known and unknown).

In the following chapters, two researchers, Marc Dantonio and Shane Sirois, not only investigate this flap, but share personal encounters of their own. Marc is MUFON's chief photo and video analyst and has served as a subject matter expert and visual effects creator on UFO programs for networks including Discovery, National Geographic, History Channel, and Science Channel. Shane is the director and founder of trueghost. com. His own near-death experience has made him the "go-to person" when hauntings get tough. He has a 100-percent success rate for resolving paranormal cases using his own unique methodology.

It's time to look at some examples of the "flap" that has been active for potentially hundreds of years or more and is still active to this day.

CHAPTER 9

MISSING TIME ON BURR POND

"Lost time is never found again."
—BENJAMIN FRANKLIN

That morning, Marc Dantonio, a bright, observant, well-adjusted school boy, clutched his brown-bag lunch as he stood more or less patiently waiting for the school bus. He was anticipating an exciting day filled with a welcome change in routine and fascinating, new experiences, as his class was scheduled for a field trip to Burr Pond. It was located at the center of the state park by the same name in Torrington, Connecticut (just up the road from Donna Fillie's farmhouse).

As the bus came into sight his excitement grew. The bus stopped. The doors folded open. He looked up inside at the smiling face of the bus driver and placed his left foot on to the bottom step preparing to board. Those were the last things the boy remembered until he found himself making his way back down those same steps at his bus stop later that afternoon. He just stood there—fully perplexed. He was quite certain that it had only been seconds before when he had entered the bus. Why would he be back there? He looked down and found the brown bag containing his lunch still clutched firmly in his hand. He looked inside. It had not been touched—never opened, never eaten.

Shocked, frightened, and feeling lost, Marc tried to force some relevant memory. His brow furrowed. His lower lip drew up and quivered ever so slightly. He found himself caught between fascination and terror, what he knew had to be real and his inability to recall a single detail

153

relating to it. He felt like crying and yet there was nothing to cry about. The prior 10 hours were represented in his mind by nothing but darkness—not so much as a fleeting image or sound or emotion.

Although he was not initially sure why, he decided to keep the experience—or lack of experience, or whatever—to himself. He didn't mention it to his parents. He even kept it private from his closest friends with whom he shared everything. He didn't ask the other students what they had done or seen that day. For some reason, not knowing seemed more comfortable at that moment—safer somehow. He didn't want to appear in any way peculiar to the others and that line of questioning seemed likely to head him directly down the path to becoming "that kid"—the oddball or outcast every youngster feared being and would do whatever seemed necessary to avoid.

So, it just sat there somewhere deep inside him: a dark, terrifying, worrisome, conundrum. Among his first thoughts, of course, was that he might be losing his mind. At his age he couldn't be certain just what that meant but, face it, time can't just vanish. There had to be some explanation. Perhaps it would all come back in the minutes and hours ahead. He'd seen it happen on TV shows—memories returning after having been lost from a blow to the head. So, he quietly carried the heavy load of that fully unexplainable experience alone.

That evening it began. His body began shaking uncontrollably. It seemed obvious to his family: Marc was having a seizure. A few minutes later he was being rushed to the hospital in an ambulance. In the emergency room the doctor agreed that it appeared to be seizure activity and the medical staff initiated treatment to stabilize the condition.

Once the obvious and dramatic symptoms were over and Marc was resting more comfortably, the doctor had several questions for him.

"Did anything out of the ordinary happen to you today? Any strange feelings, pains, or unexplainable aromas?"

Marc's mind raced. The trip! Had something happened? Who knew? In his mind, there had been no trip. In his mind there had been no "today." His plan had been to keep it all to himself. Why was the doctor interfering? It required that he provide an answer. To say "nothing" would only lead to more probing. He didn't want more probing. He opened his mouth and provided a lie, which, from his fund of generally unfounded information about such medical things, he thought should handle the question and quash further questioning.

"I fell on a dock out at Burr Pond during the field trip today. Guess I hit my head."

Rather than quieting the situation there in the hospital so he could quickly be rid of the place, it exacerbated things. After only moments of consultation, the emergency team decided that Marc needed to be treated as if he had a concussion in addition to the steps necessary to control the seizures. Epilepsy medication was prescribed. A series of "Don't Do's" was handed to his parents; keep quiet, no sudden moves, avoid bumping his head. Once that condition had been stabilized and he reported that he was feeling better (which, at that moment, was what he would have reported even if he suspected he was on his last legs), he was released from the hospital and his parents took him home.

That incident started years of what he would later determine was unnecessary epilepsy medication. During the following decade Marc experienced no hints of the condition. His doctors took that to mean the medication was working. Marc took it to mean he really didn't need the medication. Apparently Marc was correct because he stopped taking it cold turkey and never experienced a problem again. Sometimes the medical profession forgets to "see" their patients in their larger milieu and therefore misses the obvious: *Burr Pond had no docks.* That information would have shed a different light on the problem: the need for the lie and all the additional information that might have then followed.

The Burr Pond missing time incident was just the beginning of Marc's encounters with the paranormal. Years later, as an adult, doctors found a colloid cyst in his brain that needed to be removed. They operated successfully and there were apparently no after effects or complications. How long it had been there and whether or not it played any part in the Burr Pond incident is probably open for conjecture. However…

A number of significant problems occurred during the period following the surgery. Life became complicated, convoluted, and illusory. Marc had trouble working in his home office. He began hearing voices for which there were no obvious sources. He felt as though he was eavesdropping on an unseen group of people or as if there were a party going on in the room next door.

He reported those bizarre experiences to his doctor thinking they might have been some sort of aftermath from the surgery. Could they have been hallucinations induced by some aspect of the operation?

Not able to provide a conclusive answer, the doctor arranged for an MRI. The results came back normal. Marc described his visions to a number of medical specialists, all of whom said his descriptions did not match anything that would be related to his injury, the operation, or the subsequent treatment. They were at a loss to provide an answer.

The "visions" continued. What possible explanations might there be? Hallucinations seemed to accurately describe them, but of course description never answers the "why" or the "how did they come about" questions? So, if hallucinations, from what source? If not hallucinations, what other sources for the experiences might there be? Resurfaced memories, perhaps, of things he had seen years before that he simply did not remember because they were not effectively stored in his conscious mind? He decided to test that hypothesis during an event, which, from that day forward, changed Marc's view of the world—and possibly many facets or faces of the "world."

Many years after Burr Pond I had an unexplainable experience. Although the images I remember are not fully distinct, the experience is. I woke up and realized that I was having something implanted into my sinus. The "being" that was working on me had the look of an alien. I couldn't see well because I was unable to move my eyes; they were fixed, as if frozen in place. I remained fully awake throughout the procedure, which seemed to be taking place in my house. Although many things about the encounter are fuzzy, one thing is very clear: It was a terrifying event and caused me to move my family to a new home.

I went to Hartford Hospital to have whatever it was removed. I was told it was a polyp. I had a suspicion so I asked if an implant (like a piece of metal) could have a polyp form around it over time. The doctor said it was possible so I asked him to check inside the growth to see if there was something inside. At that time it was already in a jar being labeled to go to pathology.

He asked me why I had reason to suspect such a thing. Looking back I believe I made a mistake when I told him the story of being awakened several nights before by knocking noises and flashing lights at the window (the dogs never slept under the window again). I explained that I woke up totally paralyzed, unable to move my eyes, and unable to hear anything—not even my heartbeat or my own breathing.

He laughed and said he was sure it wasn't aliens. He said to give him a call in a week for the results of the biopsy.

A week later I called him and the doctor himself got on the phone as if the staff was alerted ahead of time to my call. When do you call a doctor's office and have the doctor himself get on the phone? Never. His side of the conversation was strange from the outset.

"I just want to let you know that I am sure there is nothing to it—it's benign I'm sure."

I asked for clarification.

"What do you mean, I'm sure? Did pathology give you a report?"

"Well...okay, look. This is the first time this has ever happened in my office, but I sent it to pathology and they seem to have lost it."

From his point of view that was it. The end.

I'm not a conspiracy guy, but I couldn't keep my mind from going down that path. First, it was strange that something so extraordinary would get lost and, second, that it was the first biopsy specimen that had ever been lost in his office. I didn't buy it.

Four years later, I returned to his office for something else and an interesting conversation ensued. He related that when he was younger he had been in the Air Force (in fact, he had just recently given up his top secret clearance). He explained to me that when he left the military, he entered medical school.

My mind started assembling all the bits and pieces. He still had his security clearances when he removed the polyp. When someone has a top secret clearance and something out of the ordinary comes to his attention that needs to be reported, it gets reported. If it is determined it needs to get buried, it gets buried.

Today I have no doubt that he reported the implant. There is, of course, no way to confirm that, so in reality it has to remain a suspicion. I do know what I experienced that night in my bedroom and the terror that accompanied it. Clearly, my dogs remembered it as well.

Figure 9-1. *Astrophysicist Marc Dantonio in his home office.*

CHAPTER 10

THE MOST FAMOUS CRYPTID AND A SECRET GOVERNMENT BASE

"With all the diversity of the locomotion illustrated by the creature in this footage, its gait as seen is absolutely non-typical of man."
—DR. DMITRI D. DONSKOY, CHIEF OF THE CHAIR OF BIOMECHANICS AT THE USSR CENTRAL INSTITUTE OF PHYSICAL CULTURE, MOSCOW

Summer 1997: Donna and Michelle's Sighting

We used to go there often to get a cup of coffee, just drive around, or stop to pick nuts or berries. On one occasion we were driving at night along a country road in that vicinity. We had set a leisurely pace enjoying the view in the moonlight. There were woods and pastures stretching away from the fences that framed both sides of the picturesque country road.

Presently—and at the same moment—there in the beams of our headlights, we both saw something moving beside the road, at the edge of the woods. We slowed even further to watch and try to figure out what it might be. We had a clear and unobstructed view. We saw it. We didn't understand what we were seeing, but we saw it. It was tall, taller than any animal in that area resembling, perhaps, a horse standing up on its hind legs and yet not really. It had a weird, horse-like face, which was pink-toned and bulbous toward the bottom. It was covered with long hair. Most bizarre of all, it "stood" there with his feet or hooves (neither of us could remember) some 10 feet above the ground. We had no idea of what it might be but later, when we described it to each other our visions had been identical. It made no indication that it had been aware of our intrusion—no head or body movement in our direction. We had perceived no noises from it. It provided more than a startle response for us—it scared us both to the point that we screamed and sped off down the old road.

On another occasion, while we were taking a drive in that same general area, we heard a very loud animal sound, which immediately drew our attention. We stopped to listen and soon heard it a second time. It was unlike any animal sound we had ever heard and yet we were both quite sure it *was* an animal sound.

It took place at the deep woods on the water company's property. The area has long remained unused and lies about a half mile from our house. We talked about it all the way home. In some ways it resembled the call of a moose. It was unlike anything I had ever heard in my entire life. A few nights later I heard it again—loud and clear just like it had been the first time. It seemed to have been calling from somewhere across the brook. Thinking back, it contained some elements of a scream. I have heard bobcats, raccoons fighting, weasels, coyotes, and coy dogs. Those sounds are commonplace around here where I grew up. It haunts me because it was such an unusual sound. It began as a low murmur and then raised to a much higher pitch, which it held for some time before just ceasing altogether. That night it also repeated the sound just once. I called a lady neighbor to see if she had heard it. She reported that she had. She was in her 80s and a lifelong resident of the area. She said she had never heard anything like that before either.

Bigfoot sightings go back to at least the 1950s in modern times in this area and there are legends of the sky people interacting with them here hundreds of years before. Famous sightings have taken place on this rural land and can be found on the BFRO (Bigfoot Field Researchers Organization) website under Connecticut, then Litchfield County. A famous one involving a very fast Bigfoot chasing a guy on a horse is a classic area sighting.

A Secret Government Base

"I wasn't going to give that information to Carter [on UFOs]. This was information that existed on a need-to-know basis only. Simple curiosity on the part of the president wasn't adequate."
—PRESIDENT GEORGE BUSH, SR. (WHEN DIRECTOR OF THE C.I.A.)

In 2009, the local newspaper attracted a variety of posts from local residents about UFO sightings in the immediate area. One poster attached his name and address—East Street in Goshen. The man who placed the post was the one who had been escorted off the property in question by military personnel some time before. He posted again stating that people in his neighborhood knew about an area, which he called Area 52, located not far from him. He went on to say he encouraged his fellow citizens to share with him any information they might have about it. He appeared to have been relatively new to this area at the time.

Donna's son then told her a story that bothered her. At the end of the road where the Goshen newspaper poster lives, there is a road named Sheehan-Hageman Road. It is named after the families that settled there, many of which still live in the area. The road is a dead end that stops at a huge swamp at the base of a mountain.

He is acquainted with the man who lives in the last house on that road and says there is a gate that closes off the swamp and mountain. That man, and another young man who Donna has known since he was born, went to Agricultural High School together in Litchfield. One evening while they were together at the house at the end of the road, they crossed over the property line into a clearing and built a small campfire where they were talking. Within minutes, military personnel came out of the woods with "machine guns" (their own words) and escorted them away from the area at gunpoint with pointed threats to them if they ever returned. Donna's son swears to the truth of this story. The friend who lives in that last house comes from an honest farming family with no ulterior motives. He told this story several times throughout the years. Donna's son has confirmed the story independently from his other friend who was there.

This family has also reported the existence of annoying helicopter traffic through the years. They fly in and out frequently, scaring their livestock. They have placed inquiries, but have never received an answer.

That area is extremely familiar to Donna, and after checking Google Earth, she found there were no buildings visible anywhere in the entire area. Donna's son thinks there may be some sort of underground complex there because he has also looked and has never detected any structures.

There is no regular ground traffic going in or out of that area as far as anybody reports. Numerous people continue to report having been chased out by armed military personnel. Another one of them was a friend who took a four wheeler on to the property. He told Donna that there is a tower up in there. She went on to Google Earth and found what appears to confirm that there is a tower in a swamp area in that location. Her son said that the men who escorted various people away from the area were heavily armed and were dressed in black uniforms. This person reported what others have: There are no buildings or landing areas visible from any vantage point.

Numerous other people have posted in the local newspaper that they have also been escorted off the Goshen property near Hageman Shean Road. They state that they have been grilled with questions about why they were there and what they had seen. That same experience seems to just keep recurring. People are considering taking video cameras and walking the property to find out for themselves what is up there. It is becoming the focus of interest for many people.

There is one more thing that Donna's son related to her: When he was a young teen, he was playing in a field above her house that belongs to his friend's family. They are dairy farmers. They have fields that are not accessible by foot and are, in fact, secluded and extremely difficult to find. The boys came upon a slope that faces Goshen and found on it a gigantic "T" constructed from bones. There was no hair, fur, hooves, or anything that indicated what animals the bones may have come from, but they reported it as huge. He estimated it to be somewhere between 40 to 50 feet high. Cow bones would not be sufficient to make something that big. They reported it to his friend's parents who had about 40 dairy cows, and they said that none were missing and dismissed the story, apparently without ever checking into it.

Spring 2009

Michelle and I took a ride up to Hageman Shean road in Goshen, to the farm where the guys had talked about being accosted by armed military people. We drove slowly, surveying the woods on each side of the road to see if there was anything worth reporting. We found a strange metal structure right on the side of the road. It was about 8 feet high, maybe three feet wide, and two feet deep. It appeared to be made from gray metal and had the door opened to the back of it. It was about the size of a gym locker and was attached to the ground. Its top was layered. There were no windows or antennas on it, even though in its entirety, it looked like some sort of large utility box. Portions of it displayed large rust spots. There were no wires leading to or from it that could be seen above ground. On a tree next to it was posted a yellow triangle shaped sign that said the property was protected by *Guardian*. We drove 75 feet to the farm driveway where the road turned right. Just after the turn there was a bright yellow metal gate across an overgrown road. There were tire marks going beyond it into the woods. It looked to be a road used by the farmers. We slowed down and noticed trails through the woods. There was a large cleared area way off in the distance. There are numerous swamps in that area, and that could be the case there, but we could not be sure. We followed the road past the yellow tubular gate and went on several hundred feet and took another right, circling the land where the gate was. The woods were thick and there was nothing further to be seen. I just wanted to let you know what we found from the vantage point of the road.

Summer 2009

There has been an enormous amount of military helicopter traffic during the last two days. It is all heading southeast to northwest. On Wednesday evening I heard a very loud rumbling outside and thought a huge truck had gone past the house. My daughter called from the back-yard for me to come see the plane going over. There happened to be a friend here who is an airline pilot. He identified it as a huge C130 military plane. It flew so low over our house that it cleared the trees by no more than 40 feet and rattled the windows. He was amazed because he said that FAA regulations do not allow planes to fly that low except during takeoff and landing. The plane was so low that it looked like it would not clear the trees, then it banked to the left toward Goshen. Last time there was major helicopter traffic in our area that UFO flap occurred.

The only National Guard base in our area is at Bradley International Airport in Windsor Locks. We actually turned on our police scanner and waited to hear a report of a plane crash—it was that low. Only once before have I seen a plane flying that low around here. Again, it had been a military plane, but it had come from the other direction and was flying just a bit higher. It was accompanied by two helicopters. The plane had a large glass dome on the top, accentuated by small windows. I could see the silhouettes of the pilots inside. On each occasion it had been a prop plane, not a jet.

The army corps of engineers maintains a tower on the property. The entrance to the other facility is accessed through a large farm. All vehicles and traffic that moved toward the restricted area crossed that farm's private acreage. It was located far from public access. The name of the farm was the same as the military base.

The facility was underground and all personnel wore black uniforms and regularly carried automatic weapons in plain view on and off the property. There were small convoys of black vehicles and black helicopters frequently landed on the site, although actually setting down out of view from neighboring properties.

There were no above-ground buildings and it is widely believed (although not proven) that it was an underground facility.

About three years ago, the entrances and all access to the facility were abruptly sealed and within a week the place was abandoned. There was a mass exit from the property. Apparently, all the personnel and vehicles left abruptly. The owner of the farm abandoned his property also, and his current whereabouts seem to be unknown.

The place is now protected by a skeleton crew of armed "black op" personnel who give the distinct impression that they will make it their business to keep anyone away by any means necessary.

People in the area think there was either biological, animal, or alien testing at the site and possibly something went horribly wrong, so they had to evacuate the area on the spot and seal the entrances. They are diligently protecting something. Either they want something kept inside or are afraid that something got out.

Personally, I wonder if there were people killed in the facility and they just sealed them inside. It seems like it is easy for certain people to go missing today. Anyway, whatever went on up there, they made sure it is inaccessible to the public—absolutely no way to get close enough to find out anything. No one who has come in contact with these black uniformed people dares return a second time. I guess it is so far in, and they have state-of-the-art surveillance all over the place.

~

When Paul and Ben Eno drove through that area, they found what they described as strange communicator boxes on top of the telephone poles and Paul was chased out of the area by armed military-type personnel!

Figure 10-1. *A photo of this beautiful route on a road trip the author took with Donna to view the area of military activity. It is all private property, which is fenced and locked now.*

CHAPTER 11

WHEN ARE THEY FROM?

"Whether it's a false or genuine memory, the brain's neural mechanism
underlying the recall of the memory is the same."
—PROFESSOR SUSUMU TONEGAWA

One spring evening in 2014, Daniel was driving his girlfriend along
Route 183 on the way to her house near Winchester Center. As they
rounded a curve they came upon an area just ahead that was congested
with a dozen police cars and a half dozen fire trucks. They slowed to a
near stop and viewed the scene. Large, domed, emergency lights were
swirling atop the vehicles. Another fire engine passed them and joined
the others just ahead. Firemen in full gear were heading into the woods
off to the left where flames leapt high into the air. It became apparent
they could not pass on down the road, so Daniel eased the car to where
a state trooper was standing in the middle of the road. His patrol car
looked odd; Daniel couldn't quite put his finger on it. There were none
of the usual flashing or twirling lights on it. The car was completely dark.
He called out through the open window.

The state trooper, his back to Daniel, was watching the firemen and
had not appeared to have seen the two of them in the car. Without turning to look at them, he told them to slow down because there had been
an automobile accident. They stopped and waited 10 minutes or so.
There were no pylons or other road barriers as would have been expected at the sight of a major accident. No one offered them any information
or provided any further directions. They were left to their own devices.
Daniel turned the car around. The officer's uniform seemed odd, too.

In fact, the whole setting seemed odd. In the confusion, Daniel couldn't put it together, but he had been around police all his life and things just didn't seem right.

Everything about the situation seemed out of sync—the language pattern of the policeman, his lack of direct attention to them, and the vehicles; the fire trucks with rounded fenders and hoods extending out front of the cabs; the ancient-looking twirling lights; and even the police cars that looked as if they were out of some classic car parade. The whole situation spooked both Daniel and his girlfriend. She scooted closer to him and put her arm through his.

Daniel and his girlfriend shared several possible explanations: Maybe there was a period movie being shot there—out of the Forties, perhaps. That idea didn't stand up to even a moment's scrutiny; there were no lights or cameras or movie support people. It remained a mystery—an eerie, unexplainable mystery. She clutched Daniel's arm even tighter.

The young man followed the road to their left. It was an area with which they were familiar. Why, then, did the territory seem strange? He should have been able to travel those roads without having to think about it. That was not the case. What was wrong?

He slowed to a stop on a relatively untraveled dirt road with some houses on it leading into the woods.

"Let's see if that road will get us back on track."

His girlfriend nodded in agreement.

He turned and followed the road straight through the woods away from the accident, but in the end they found themselves back to where they had started. They both knew where they were. If they continued on that road they would soon arrive back at the scene of the accident. The whole experience was unnerving and Mary burst into tears.

He turned right, which should have taken them back to the exact location where they had encountered the cars and trucks and the fire and the state policeman. There was not a police car in sight! All the emergency vehicles were gone. There was no fire and no charred trees to indicate there had ever been one. The entire scene as they both remembered it had vanished like it had never happened.

It could not have been a figment of the imagination—they had *both* witnessed it. They both had emotional reactions to it and felt an unexplainable, unnerving confusion about it lingering on within them.

The two continued to his girlfriend's house in silence and went inside with the strange and confusing emergency scene stuck in the forefront of their minds. They provided a brief description of the incident to her parents and, at the suggestion of her father, they went immediately to Google Earth and retraced their exact route, hoping to begin making sense of it. How could all of that have suddenly vanished, leaving no trace behind?

Google confirmed the route taken was exactly as previously expected. Thinking back, they determined there had been no cell service during the whole experience and that had never been a problem on that stretch of road before. Later inquiry of others who had been in that area at about the same time provided no information that would tend to substantiate what the young people reported. There were no television, radio, or newspaper reports of an accident on that road.

Of the several possible explanations for what happened to Daniel and his girlfriend, one could relate to a UFO abduction. There are many references in existence that report people returning from such an experience with gaps in their memories—as if significant portions of the experiences they had were wiped clean. Still other reports suggest that replacement memories may have been supplied by the "aliens" so that gap would be filled and the time away seemed less out of the ordinary. (Remove those new memories, which the aliens cannot allow the person to retain, but provide substitute memories which ostensibly fill that time period—memories that should make sense.)

It is possible that those replacement memories may sometimes be inaccurate representations of life on Earth based on imprecise observations by the aliens. In the case of Daniel and his girlfriend, had they been abducted and their brains wiped clean, the replacement memories could have been borrowed from a period in history that appeared oddly inaccurate in the process. The police cars, the uniforms, and the vehicles of the policemen and fire department drawn from an era just past, in that example, could be examples of such alien inaccuracies. One hundred years in Earth time might well seem like a mere second in their time frame.

It has long been held that erasing and replacing memories in the human brain is an unlikely if not impossible process and that contention has been used to cast doubt on such reports. Recent physiological ~~search in the brains of mice, however, suggests otherwise. False memories have indeed been implanted in test animals. In fact, they worked so well that they completely incapacitate the animals in conditions their real life circumstances suggested should not have occurred. This new research certainly substantiates the possibility that extraterrestrials could, indeed, do the same in humans (Xu Lio and Steve Ramirez, in *Science*, 2013).

Chapter 12

Other Haunted Houses

"If one thinks to look, it is usually never just the one house
in an area that is experiencing the paranormal."
—Paul F. Eno

In this paranormal flap, there are many disturbances taking place throughout the years. Here are a few examples:

Neighbor 1

A nearby neighbor of Donna's had a suicide in their house in 1940. A man threatened to kill his entire family and set the house on fire. Instead, he threw all their stuff out of the house, took a gun, and shot and killed himself. These neighbors have phenomena, too, such as footsteps and activity up and down their staircase.

Neighbor 2

"After my husband passed, there was music that could be heard from the basement. That is where my husband played his guitar. I could hear it as being muffled and it was classical rock music like he used to play. Exact songs couldn't be heard because it was muffled as if behind closed doors. I used to go in the basement looking to see if there was a radio on somewhere. I would hear it in the kitchen or living room, but in my bedroom I couldn't hear it and we had grates there. It would last five to seven minutes—ten at the most—every day for about a year and a half. Then it stopped.

"About a year and a half ago, I would come home and the covers would be pulled down (I make the bed every morning and closed the door). No one went in there. This happened not every day but about four days a week. It only happened on my side of the bed. Those sheets would be turned down perfectly. In August of 2014 that stopped. I feel that my husband finally realized that I am okay now. I have had a lot of stress with my daughter. Occasionally there is something moved here or there, but no more of the other phenomena.

"I am finally able to be independent again. I can keep the house and now I can manage it all and I am doing it. I think he sees it and feels it and can let go. I feel inner peace. I haven't been this happy in so long. My husband was sick for five years before he passed. He had liver cancer.

"My father passed in 1996 and my mother passed in 2002. I used to think I was half asleep because my dad would talk to me and say it would be okay, then my mother talked to me and my father stopped. In tough times, I still hear from her.

"One Friday night, I had a great day at work and when I went to bed I could feel that she was there and she whispered and said 'feeling good.' I always had these weird instances. I heard from my girlfriend that passed away for at least a year. I believe it is possible to still be in touch and have those connections with loved ones who pass on."

Neighbor 3

One neighbor that owns a small hobby farm had the door blow open during a storm and there were wet footsteps going down the hall. This all happened when there was no one else in the house.

Neighbor 4

Another neighbor has UFO sightings outside in his yard. He is certain they are not planes or stars. The movement is unusual because they stand still and then they go behind the trunk of a tree and then come back out. He tracks the flight patterns and insists they are not planes.

There are many well-known rumored haunted spots that are out of scope of our investigation. For those that would like a handy list, here are a few of these places: Warner Theater (Torrington, CT), Mohawk

Mountain (Cornwall, CT), Dudleytown (Cornwall, CT), Hillside Cemetery (Cheshire, CT), James Alldis House (Torrington, CT), Oak Avenue (Torrington, CT), Yankee Peddler Inn (Torrington, CT), and Dennis Hill State Park (Norfolk, CT).

PART III

INVESTIGATION, THEORY, AND DISCUSSION

Chapter 13

Paranormal Assumptions

"A few years ago, the city council of Monza, Italy, barred
pet owners from keeping goldfish in curved bowls...saying that
it is cruel to keep a fish in a bowl with curved sides because, gazing
out, the fish would have a distorted view of reality. But how do we
know we have the true, undistorted picture of reality?"
—Stephen Hawking

Chapter Disclaimer

The information in this chapter may make some readers uncomfortable. It may make others angry. Don't be. Suspend any initial defensive stance. Receive the information and take from it what you will. Who am I to tell you definitively what the "truth" is about such things? Think of this as an opportunity for us to think together about how our vision can be narrowed when we experience or attempt to interpret these sorts of phenomena. Each of us tends to interpret things from our own unique vantage point based on our own unique fund of information and experiences. All of that is influenced by our needs and fears and other predispositions. The conclusions we draw about what may or may not lay beyond the veil is inevitably clouded or clarified by all of these things. Consider the following topics.

Hoax scrutiny and declarations

As a magician, I require that accusations of a hoax be proven. Agendas are everywhere, and public declarations are in need of careful scrutiny, too. The UFO field saw this run rampant with Philip Klass's incorrect statements based on lack of research of the facts. The famous Bigfoot Peddleton video also faced cries of hoax but has never actually been proven to be a hoax, but it has puzzled scientists that tried to discredit it, yet looked closer at the film and the movements of the creature. Even Hollywood couldn't duplicate it with a "suit." Yet misinformation and public declaration ruled the day. In fact, I am very shocked that I often see more misinformation and abuse of the facts by those trying to prove something is a hoax than by those who believe it is real phenomena! How do we avoid this? Let's just use the same methodology. Don't guess, don't lie, and your opinions are just that—opinions. They are fine and welcome, as long as they are clearly labeled as such. Let's stick to the facts and detail them. However, the "don't lie" part is a challenge.

Ghosts of the dead?

It is natural for us to assume that if we see a "spirit" of someone that we know is "dead," then they are appearing from "beyond" or the afterlife. Like most of our primitive assumptions, we divide things into two— here and there—which we call "beyond." Although an obvious and very common correlation, it may be true. However, it is far from being a definitive theory. In the theory of the multiverse, it would also make sense. What if spirits who couldn't cross over needed to cross back over to their familiar world and not to a one-dimensional other world or spirit world? What if they were very much alive and we are being given a glimpse into an otherwise-hidden view of the multiverse?

In more than 30 years of investigation into so-called talking to the dead, I have never been presented with any evidence or even confirmation that a deceased loved one departed valuable information that only they would know. I am not talking about through a medium who can research such matters easily to confirm the known, but from the deceased to the loved one or family. In my mind, this doesn't mean that all of these experiences are frauds. It does suggest, however, that perhaps we are witnessing limited communication due to a parallel world intersect. If they are in fact living a different life in a different world, they wouldn't be inclined to depart things of this nature. Sometimes they wouldn't even communicate directly with you.

Here are two quotes that I particularly find fascinating in the discussion:

I don't believe that ghosts are "spirits of the dead" because I don't believe in death. In the multiverse, once you're possible, you exist. And once you exist, you exist forever one way or another. Besides, death is the absence of life, and the ghosts I've met are very much alive. What we call ghosts are life forms just as you and I are.
—Paul F. Eno

When I see ghosts they look perfectly real and solid—like a living human being. They are not misty; I can't see through them; they don't wear sheets or bloody mummy bandages. They don't have their heads tucked under their arms. They just look like ordinary people, in living color, and sometimes it is hard to tell who is a ghost.
—Chris Woodyard

Delayed crossing

Those who have passed *on* but "feel" they are not yet ready can delay their crossing *over* to the other side until they are ready. Think of these "souls" as the same kids that didn't finish their homework when it was due and the teacher gave each one more chances to complete it. Those who suffered through it late into the night to make sure it was done on time got no extra reward for their diligence. I theorize that there is much more to this regardless of your belief system. "I am not ready" never cut it with the nuns for me in Catholic grammar school and I don't think it is an acceptable reason for a delay after we die (or appear to die) in the visible here and now.

An after death experience

"I have no GPS. I am lost. Even in death, I have difficulty finding my way."

Most who die manage to take care of themselves and get to where they need to go. Not these folks. They wander around aimlessly hoping to find an arrow to direct their way. Even in death they can't get it right. If they are lucky, a medium among the living will help them complete their passage since they are helpless on their own. (I have the definite feeling that I will end up in this class of wandering "spirits." I get lost right here on the well-mapped earth. Imagine my plight within the unknown?)

I never thought that this made any sense. It does make sense that tragedies or intense emotions are perhaps one way to "open" a view or form a parallel world intersect (or substitute your theory or belief system here), but to me getting lost is a sign of getting stuck between. That between does not appear to be a traditional purgatory belief. If souls get stuck, lost, and displaced, one starts to wonder what kind of operation God is running up there. Why are people able to get displaced or lost? This is a wondrous area to ponder and discuss.

An interpretation of the not fully understood

If something acts in some way that is perceived as negative, then its whole being must be evil. We throw the word *evil* around a lot in paranormal discussions and once that label is attached to a force or essence it tends to define its complete, singular property. This position grows directly out of the human being's need for self-preservation; if we can't be sure something is completely safe, we tend to classify it as potentially hurtful and do not approach it. We often seek to destroy the unknown as a result of this preservation approach. I'll never forget the words in an episode of *The Outer Limits*. A person steps on a spider and the other person asks them if they know why they did it. Hearing no answer, he responds back, "We kill what we don't understand," which is why we fear the unknown so much. As the old saying goes, "Things can always get worse."

If another species observed us and our actions during times of extreme behavior brought upon by fear, being away from home, feeling we are under attack, mental illness, confusion, and the like, they might reach the same conclusion that we are evil.

My mom always taught me that first impressions mean everything. It's true. An entity displays negative behavior and we will categorize their whole being as being that way. And why not? Corporate America does the same. One wrong action could make it so you will never advance. Years ago, a neck tattoo used to hold back your promotion by about five years. A nose ring could hold it back for who knows how long. If we are so harsh to judge our own species even after getting to know them and their work ethic, it's only natural that we categorize the unknown in very strict compartments even though we only see them in a limited capacity and probably not even at their best.

Multiverse questions

If there was a multiverse, Jesus would have told us all about it in the Bible.

They can't be entities from another world because the Bible calls them demons. Let's face it: Primitive humans require primitive explanations. Why would we expect anything else? The paranormal holds up to all religions. You can even be an atheist and believe in the paranormal. The reasons behind it are where we will all differ but that is an open discussion that no one can definitively solve as of today.

It's always about us

We never seem to consider the entities' point of view. I am not saying that things are not always as they seem. Sometimes, they are exactly as they seem. The challenge with the paranormal is that there are so many unknowns, we limit ourselves when we label phenomena and only accept that it can be one way.

One example I like to use is possession. We universally think about possession from the point of view that something else is invading us on purpose and taking over our body as an evil act. For the purposes of our discussion, let's ignore all the psychological behaviors that can be cured by a fake ceremony, or those instances that can be cured by ignoring the person altogether.

The common view of possession involves ourselves as the center. It's all about us. This is no surprise because that is the way we view our world. Everything revolves around us. We even once thought it actually did planet-wise.

What if possession really is an entity finding itself inside a person? Not deliberately, but it just ends up there? Now it is scared, angry, fighting from the inside. Evil? Maybe or maybe not. But suddenly, in this example, it's not just about us anymore. It is something that has happened to two beings, not one. This is a tough theory for anyone to consider. We are the good things minding our own business and it's these things that are the bad guys. They are evil. Completely evil. Really? And how well do we know them? From a religious point of view, we would say they are demons. However, we don't know what these things are. We do know they "visit" people of all faiths and they can always be dispelled without the use of any religion. The bottom line is that these various entities are simply not the theologians we thought they were.

And the most shocking assumption of all...

Once we die, all the answers will be revealed to us. This would nicely fulfill our need for closure and for everything to neatly fit into place, wouldn't it? Not only is life made fair in the afterlife, but we expect to finally have it all figured out.

However, this is the biggest paranormal assumption of all beliefs. The reality is there may be no first-day orientation afterward and as our spirit, soul, or energy (or insert whatever you believe) lives on, you may be as clueless about many things as you are today. Or perhaps more so.

Chapter 14

What Magic Has Taught Me About Interpreting the Paranormal

"Which is more likely? That the universe was designed just for us, or that we see the universe as having been designed just for us?"
—Michael Shermer

Our mind looks for connections. We are always looking for connections. It is what we do. It is how we are wired. When we see one thing and something else appears, we do our best to connect the two.

To illustrate: We look for connections between and among faces. We tend to feel immediate connections with certain faces. With others, we don't. It happens even though we are typically not aware of it. Why is that? There are several reasons, one of which is that we might know or have known someone else who resembles the face in terms of structure, form, and coloration. If we remember them as a nice, safe or comfortable person, it is likely we will believe that same thing about the second person. Looking for these connections is part of our basic survival mechanism—separating the safe from the unsafe. It is a trait we share with other animals who, often as a matter of life and death, have to determine friend from foe—fight or flight—very quickly.

Extending this principle to magic, it suggests that if a magician takes a broken object, covers it, waves his hand, and then reveals an unbroken object that looks like the first, we will conclude that a restoration of that first object has taken place. It never enters our mind that perhaps the magician somehow got rid of the broken version of the object and made a new unbroken version appear. A vanish of item "A-1" followed by an appearance of item "A-2" is not what our mind concludes or perceives.

183

Why? Because we look for (need, actually) *connections.* Our mind prefers consistency and continuation. We want our world to make sense in the simplest possible ways. *One* object restored is simpler than *two* objects anyway you cut it! So, we strive to make pieces fit.

When we see something *broken* and then see an apparently identical something *not broken* in the same place, our mind concludes that the single object has been restored.

Now, modify the very same magic trick just a bit and have one object vanish from a table and then appear somewhere else, and our mind will still connect those two events (objects) as one. We see it as an illusion of transportation—teleportation. The object was over here on the table and now *that same object* is over there. In this example, our mind focuses on the placement of *the single* object. We don't consider that may have involved the vanishing of one item and an appearance of another relatively identical item. The simplest connection tends to win.

So, a magician can combine "a vanish" and "an appearance" and make (allow) the audience perceive that an item has been restored from its broken condition, or has be teleported across space. Employing the same general approach, the audience can also witness it as time travel by having the object, which has been moved from its original place, vanish and then appear back where it was originally—before the trick began. It is as if the moment of time has been started all over again. Even though it is still the same display, when it is presented as time travel, it will be perceived and experienced as time travel. The human mind is eager to accept any data that supports its need to believe that the simplest connection *is fact,* and magicians are masters at providing that supportive data.

My point is that the very same set of phenomena can (will) be interpreted, perceived, and experienced in multiple ways depending on the context (the supportive data) in which it exists or is presented. An individual's interpretation of the phenomena will be based on how one connects things in his own mind. When Paul Eno noted that outdoor phenomena is more often connected to UFOs and indoor phenomena is more connected to other paranormal experiences, that is a perfect example of the way our mind connects and interprets phenomena in different contexts.

But, as demonstrated, those connections, and thus an individual's interpretation of them, may not be an accurate assessment of what *actually* took place. The mind is "built" to seek comfortable explanations first, and truth second. The magician skillfully utilizes those human traits in creating illusions. In the real world it often happens just by chance, driven in that case not by the magician's skill in setting our expectations, but by the contexts or expectations we bring to situations ourselves. In either case, what may be most comfortably perceived as a single event may actually be several. Our minds often don't perceive the number of events involved correctly because they are focused on making meaningful, comfortable, uninterrupted connections instead.

I contend that in our perceptions of the paranormal world, our minds often make connections in ways that are based on these same principles. As a result, I believe our perceptions of things that may most easily be construed as paranormal are often inaccurate—*simple* rather than *true*. It is a matter of connections and is based in those things that bring a person to make one set of connections rather than some other. As a result, individuals necessarily perceive the same events differently whether they are faces, vases, or ghostly phenomena. And that is the very same reason that we would naturally interpret seeing a "spirit" of someone who is dead as seeing them as someone in the "world beyond" rather than perhaps the fact that they are very alive and being seen in a rare glimpse into another universe.

My goal here is to suggest that all those traits and beliefs and characteristics that combine to make us who we are work together to color our conclusions, our connections, and our interpretations. We may perceive the paranormal quite incorrectly because of what we know, believe, and most importantly, perhaps, don't know. We each make assumptions, which are dependent upon all those things that make us who we are: a unique individual.

CHAPTER 15

ANALYSIS OF THE PHENOMENA

"There are things known and there are things unknown,
and in between are the doors of perception."
—ALDOUS HUXLEY

Donna's Thoughts

I grew up around a lot of young people dying and escaped death many times myself. I had cancer surgery when I was six months old. My car was crushed by a falling tree while Michelle and I were in it. It destroyed the car, but we didn't receive a scratch. Michelle thought we were dead until a police officer began speaking with us. I also got kicked in the face by a horse and would have died if I had been hit just slightly differently.

So, this continuing mind game of being surrounded by death is getting old. Actually, it was old 25 years ago. I want some closure. That's one reason I don't want to leave this house. I want to know what is going on here. You would think after 40 years I would have some substantial understanding or least some promising clues.

There are questions I would like to ask our "visitors." Why do you have to knock over a salt shaker? Do you think I am supposed to know what that means? Why don't you just come out and say something or ask something? If you can do all these things, then why not do things that actually communicate something?

My mother's missing ring returned to the jewelry box. I believe she thought it was my grandmother making good on her promise to take something she normally couldn't get a hold of and putting it in a place where my mother would know who did it. My mother and I would sit down after my father went to work and we would compare notes. We'd talk about how sometimes she would hear something and ask if I had heard the same thing. Sometimes I had and sometimes I hadn't. She would discreetly call the neighbors and ask if they had heard any explosions. She was, also, interested in finding out what was going on around here, but my father would shush most discussions on the subject. He reported that he had witnessed my grandfather standing in the milk house years after his death. He reacted in a calm manner about the incident. Perhaps it was that at that point he felt he knew in his heart how things really were so he saw no reason to be upset by the rest of it. On the other hand, maybe he remained uncertain and just wouldn't acknowledge the "happenings" because that would be admitting it was all real.

I have spent years thinking about all the unusual things. Each comes back to the question of "why?" Why do the curtains lift straight in the air and lash out at my face? Clearly I know you're here, but I don't know who you are or what you want, so why do you keep doing what you are doing? I am looking at it from a logical perspective. It is trying to get my attention. It gets my attention. But then it never follows through letting me know *why* it wanted my attention. Exasperating!

I have never liked to call them ghosts. Why? My mind has evolved over the years from thinking it is a dead relative or spirit to believing it involves other non-human, leaping things. Really, though, I continue to find myself at the point of just not knowing.

I suppose the multiverse theory is possible and would explain much of what is going on here. It seems entirely plausible. Although that could account for many of the events, I tend to doubt if it explains the voices or the orbs or the door shaking. The entities we have seen—the non-human ones—like the one standing in the vanity, was clearly out of sync with space and time. And the entity that leaped by the doorway. I felt sorry for it. I felt like it was sad—cowering and sad. It was nothing I had ever seen before. I do believe in the multiverse, but I don't think it explains everything.

I think the rest of it could just be energy, like when the spoons bent, as opposed to an entity deliberately bending the spoons. I saw orbs with my own eyes. Maybe that is ghost energy. I think our electronic devices today are making parts of this phenomena more obvious and therefore more real. We have cell phones, cell towers, satellites, etc. all sending and receiving high frequency.waves that may in some ways be riling things up. I have all these theories running around in my head and all of them have the single purpose of answering why. Sometimes when I hear something I get the distinct feeling that it is trying to communicate with me. And other times I feel I am just witnessing something in a detached, more side-by-side way. Unseen dishes rattle. Could that be something that is somehow being reestablished from 100 years ago? It just doesn't make sense to me and I don't like things that don't make sense.

There is a Native American site nearby, but none of us outsiders know exactly where it is. The tribal leaders don't want to tell us, fearing vandalism. At the base of the mountain (Stillwater), all sorts of Native American artifacts were found—arrowheads and other items. I don't know if that somehow plays into all this.

I started this journal for that very reason: to try to make sense of it. And here it is today and I still can't make sense of it. I had white sage going all over this house, had the place blessed, talked to visitors, and none of it matters. It just keeps going on. I would never have a séance here and I would never use a Ouija board here. I am convinced that whatever is here has settled in because we did not call it out or encourage it. The other issue is that new entities can be let in by doing such things.

Others have suggested that this house or this immediate territory is like a meeting place—an inter-dimensional meeting place. If true, I don't want to encourage that. I want peace and quiet, not a bus station. Overhearing is fine. But I don't want to call them out and try to invite something else in here or bring anything to another level. We have what we have here and that is more than enough for me. White sage just stunk and it didn't work. Neither did the blessings.

I was lying in bed and I wondered why we have never heard anything in the attic. It's basically just two large rooms. The kitchen was a general store. Years ago, we used to close doors for protection—to keep "them" out. How silly is that? They go through doors and walls and floors.

It's impossible to get the big picture on all of this. Everyone has pieces of it, but I can't get the whole story on what all this is and how it all fits and works together. No one claims to know.

I try to eliminate all other possibilities—even today—to differentiate between ordinary happenings and the actual "phenomena." Everybody who protested about going public with the story of this house is dead and gone, so I simply don't care to protect it any longer. People who know me know about it. Many of them express interest in sleeping over, but these phenomena don't work on demand. You can be here an hour and experience it or be here for a week and see, feel, or hear nothing out of the ordinary.

Paul Eno's Thoughts

The significance of the house number

Donna's life, from the long-run perspective, pretty much centered on the address of the house in which she lived for such a large part of her life. What better "hook" for an entity to find than that when they were trying to connect or communicate or be noticed by her? It is most likely one of many, many aspects of her life that have been tried. She tuned in on the number and once she did, she became sensitive to it, so she tended to notice it when it was "sent her way." It is not necessarily a commonly reported experience, but it does occur in the literature.

The preoccupation with jewelry

Throughout Donna's accounts runs what appears to be a preoccupation with jewelry by the forces at work. Metal tends to draw these sorts of phenomena to it. They seem to rotate around it the same way they do around bathrooms, kitchens, and plumbing—all defined in some ways by metal. In such cases there may be no specific entity involved. It may, rather, just be energy swirling in the area—energy that in some ways alters the physical laws as we generally understand them. "In the case of Goodins' experience (see *The World's Most Haunted House, The True Story of the Bridgeport Poltergeist on Lindley Street*), the energy swirled right around me and yet I felt the presence of no one in the room with me." When a bioelectrical field becomes present, any person in its vicinity will sense it—feel it.

Floating globules of light: UFO or something else?

A prevailing interpretation of UFO phenomena regards the sightings as balls of light—the precise physics of which is still somewhat elusive. Whether seen up in the sky or inside a house, those orbs may be identical occurrences. It often comes down to a matter of context. One observes large floating objects in the night sky and they are easily interpreted as flying objects—how else could they be there? It only makes sense. Inside a house, especially one that is prone to exhibit unexplainable entities or occurrences, a common or reasonable interpretation would be a ghost or some related thing. These orbs, big or small, close or far, have the capacity to change—to modify themselves in shape and color and direction and speed of movement. There properties and behaviors could be interpreted as intelligent. In some ways they act like similar to ball lighting. Electromagnetic energy holds the whole multiverse together. This class of entities seems to have changed over the years. The orbs reported in the 1970s, if found at all, are different in appearance from orbs like the ones Donna and others have described recently. Light phenomenon specialists in photo labs contend that orbs are still an open question. They are all open questions.

Childlike figure with elongated ears

The vast array of things and forces reported by Donna in and around her house represent the greatest paranormal menagerie that I have run into in the last 44 years. It is therefore difficult or impossible to draw conclusions about the makeup or ultimate source of all of them. The childlike figure with the elongated ears falls within this category. Just because it has never been cataloged before should not be reason to disbelieve in its existence.

[Paul reported that he had never had a case where there were so many different life forms reported in such a confined area with appearances being so consistent through the decades.]

Knives and spoons bent in half

That is common. Their positive nature sort of keeps things in balance in a strange way. Bob and Donna are very positive people. A lot of it has to do with the people and how they react and interact with the experience.

Babies detecting entities

Young children are play- and fantasy-oriented. The boundary between real and other worldly is thin and often nearly nonexistent. That is all normal. So when approached by a paranormal entity the child will accept the newcomer on face value. To have children interact with these phenomena is well documented in the literature. Dale conversed with things in the corner and seemed to become the focus of levitation. He had his special friend—not experienced by others—who stayed with him for some time.

[Paul had a case in Florida in which there was a young boy who reported invisible friends and he actually met them. Genuine, verified, conversations occurred with them. Perhaps adults who never lose their inner child are naturally more sensitive to such happenings. Part of it is having an open attitude that can put off the adult trappings of doubt about all things that do not follow the established laws of the universe. Some children seem to be able to communicate with both positive and negative aspects of other worlds. Our concern should be reserved for the fear-or harm-producing encounters.]

Money falling in the car when Bob needed it

Sometimes coincidence becomes interpreted as a cause and effect event. The best explanation for the coins appearing in Bob's car is perhaps some combination of coincidence and paranormal energy interacting with the metal involved—that particular car and the coins. Beyond that any answer would be conjecture masquerading as wisdom.

Cigar smoke

The sense of smell is the most powerful of the senses, making it one likely to link our brain with places, people, and memories, and that either involved that aroma or could have involved that aroma. Such phenomena are commonly associated with events such as Donna and her family report. That brain-based explanation is perhaps the most likely one.

White light leaving a darkened area on the painting

[That was a first for Paul. His educated deduction is that it is in some way related to the ball light—the orbs—that became so common. The vast amount of electrical energy necessarily associated with orbs may well have made some minimal (perhaps heat-induced) transformation on the surface of the painting while the light configuration remained in contact with it. It was not entirely a surprise that it could have been the case, because while in the basement of Donna's house the investigator's compass spun wildly, suggesting an extreme excess of electrical energy.]

Michelle relating her "prior life"

This is not at all an uncommon revelation both in children and adults. In some ways it seems to be similar to the Ashwar invisible play-mate story. It has been accounted for by several things, perhaps most typically, ancestral memory. The mechanics of such experiences are not established, perhaps because it follows laws of some other realm that merely spill over occasionally in the form of such memories. [Paul finds such reports absolutely fascinating. He enjoys listening to children talk about such things and believes it is relatively easy to sense when their stories are sincere.]

Entity with a black hat and funny old clothes

This is archetypal like other figures. Some of the others that were reported include the man with the checkered shirt and the little blonde girl with flowers in her hair. A black shadow figure with a broad-brimmed hat like this is quite common. At the center of a paranormal flap, like where Donna lived, an endless variety of "things" can pass through on a single occasion and never be seen or sensed again.

Chiming clock that is broken

Broken items that suddenly begin working are very common. Typically no "reason" based in the laws of known physics can explain it, but then, in the realms of the unknown, those laws also remain unknown. It is fascinating to wonder about how processes common only to one realm may become manifest in another, if only for the briefest of moments.

Baby heard crying in the back seat of Donna's mom's car

It is reported that there is a cemetery in which you can at times hear a baby crying. This is, more generally, not unusual. The unsatisfactory explanation states that the baby may have died in the area—period. By itself that is, of course, no explanation at all. When dealing with the paranormal, however, we must often concede our ignorance up-front. If flaps exist which allow mingling between realms and times, hearing crying from the baby who died in that area is not implausible.

Missed notes

It is extremely rare to have a meaningful modification of something in order to exchange a specific message, such as writing a note that had never existed before as we saw in the Betty and Fred incident with Donna. The reports of phone calls and notes are therefore significant and very interesting. It is exciting to find that Donna and her family have unity and contact among the community of worlds. That suggests the possibility of meaningful communication—using what appears to be a mutually understood system.

Exploding plate

This event is most likely *not* an intentional act perpetrated by any entity, but rather the result of the energy suddenly overflowing on to that spot in some unconventional manner. It is interesting—at least entertaining—to speculate that energies from several realms might have converged at that spot for just long enough for their combined force to do damage.

Levitation

Levitation is not unusual. The interesting aspect of it is less in the act and more in the result. Does it merely occur in some benign fashion or does it become helpful or destructive? One of the things scrutinized in Donna's case had to do with the distribution of negative phenomena. Investigators are especially interested in determining whether or not the "energy" is manifested as hostile and destructive forces. If, in fact, some sort of levitation had been involved in returning lost objects, that would be an example of a helpful force.

Energy in the basement

Ben calls such figures "clerics." He characterized them as good and helpful neighbors. They are tall and very good natured. They appear to be looking out for people or even other beings. Perhaps it is similar to people in our realm volunteering in a soup kitchen or at animal shelters.

Shane Sirois's Thoughts

The significance of the house number

With numbers, it could be that they are frequently used or required numbers that sit at the ready in Donna's mind. Since the universal phone number for help, 911, has come into our lives in that horrific act of terrorism, people tend to see it many places it isn't—on clocks, for example. When the mind cannot collect all the data it needs to fill out a perception, it often, all quite willy-nilly, supplies data it holds in reserve, whether or not it may be logically connected. So, the most familiar sets of numbers one maintains—like house numbers, phone numbers, combinations, identity numbers, safety-related numbers—become the most likely candidates to appear. The likelihood of "seeing" any given set of numbers increases with the number of times it pops up. Eventually, such a set may become the mind's choice to fill in a memory or perception. There remains the chance, of course, that it could be an actual connection or attempt by an entity at simple communication.

The preoccupation with jewelry

It is frequently reported that entities take items and hide them. Frequent targets are things such as money, jewelry, and even remote controls! The human interpretation tends to be that such things are either done as a prank or to get attention. They want to establish a connection between the two parallels and these are apparently methods they can use or find to be successful. Attempts to communicate are drastically different from attempts to cause harm. This family's approach is really good because the door is open and bad things as well as good can enter. It has not, however, dwelled just on the bad as is so often the case. Generally positive environments, like Donna and her family have established, seem to welcome positive, non-malevolent forces and entities. Dysfunctional families, like the one in the Lindley Street case, invite the negative and they come and they stay and they feed and grow on the negativity.

Are the lights in the room consistent with UFO phenomena?

Lights, in numerous forms and levels of activity, are commonly found. Some remain stationary while others maintain some level of activity. In some cases lights have been found to possess heat, enough to warm cold pavements. [Shane has witnessed lights above people's heads inside the house when he began to interview them. On occasion it has taken a form resembling sparks or little fireworks coming from their head.]

Childlike figure with elongated ears

When a family has established that nondiscriminatory open door, the way Donna's has, anything can make its way through. They will pop in sometimes as if to merely check things out and see what is going on. Perhaps others enter in search of a playmate that will play in the manner they want to play. There seems to be an intelligence about these beings. They can tailor make their approach and their form or appearance depending on what they believe will garner their target's attention. If appearing as an adult doesn't get attention, then maybe a little girl in a nice blue dress will. In ways similar to human predators, these entities hone their skills until they can successfully enter this world and have it meet their need or needs.

Knives and spoons bent in half

The phenomenon of bent utensils is relatively rare. Certain electromagnetic frequencies can cause metal to be deformed or melt. Most assuredly, some powerful energy force is at work when it takes place. In scientific experiments, such metal bending processes have been demonstrated. Not knowing what we do and don't know about the other realms, there is no reason not to believe such events might have a paranormal basis. It would always do well to search out explanations in the here and now, first.

Babies detecting entities

Babies, children, and animals remain perceptive in ways most adults are not. As we mature and move on from days of fantasy and make-believe we tend to lose contact with certain senses that are innately associated with those processes. We also acquiesce to the expectations of the adult world we have been taught to know and believe exists. Even when and if we continue to possess those skills we tend to override them in the service of satisfying our expectations, so we may miss that which a few decades before we would have seen and embraced.

Money falling in the car when Bob needed it

[When we need something it often seems to be provided. Shane said it happen to him as a kid. His family grew up poor. His main source of enjoyment came from playing baseball. He would throw the ball against the brick wall that encircled the church. On one occasion he threw it on top of the church roof where it stayed. It was his only ball. He was saddened and just looked up at the sky, grinding his teeth. Presently, he saw some tiny object dropping at him from above. As it grew larger and larger he could see it was a ball. It dropped right into the boy's glove! It was a tennis ball rather than a baseball. It clearly had no relationship with the lost ball and yet, there it was, just when he needed it.]

Cases have been reported elsewhere in which money appeared when people really needed it. When such things occur away from home it gives credence to the belief that it is not the house that is haunted, but the person. Had it been the house such a thing could not have taken place in the car miles away. Such "money-gaining" events may involve either or both positive and negative (nasty) hauntings.

White light leaving a darkened area on the painting

It is a phenomenon that I have not experienced before.

Michelle relating her "prior life"

Although prior life experiences are frequently reported, the fact of returning from some "other side" cannot be proved. It is therefore hard to theorize beyond recording and reporting the experiences. The evidence is anecdotal. The gist of the stories is similar enough to warrant consideration. People who report such experiences often hold facts and images that were only known or present in the past or are in some other way unavailable to that person from first-hand experiences in the here and now. They may be able to name people in a picture that they have never met or been told about. Within the theories and positions of those who study the paranormal, alternate explanations may be possible. Some might propose that the information was transmitted in dreams, thinking that during sleep the mind may be open to communication from other realms or times. Others might suggest that it could also be their own ability to pick up on something that happened to somebody else who is present with them—some sort of memory reading.

[Shane reports that when his children were born, every single one of them had visitors of the paranormal variety. Some were silhouettes that moved objects in the room and continually turned on the baby monitor. When he was sick, he also had visitors from a family that he had never known. During those periods accurate information was acquired about them—looks, dress, and other features—that he later confirmed as being true with the family.]

Chiming clock that is broken

Broken items starting to work are very common phenomena. The literature is filled with examples. Frequently, physical explanations cannot be supplied.

Missing notes

It may be that entities do things like that to bring a topic to your attention—one they believe you need to be focusing on. Some would suggest that this is some kind of time travel or time slip. When a strong environment has been established, like the one in Donna's case, it becomes so active that time slip events occur. It may useful to think of these sorts of things in terms of quantum physics. It would suggest that there is something in the environment that is causing it.

Exploding plate

Although very interesting, there is virtually nothing in the literature that seems relevant. In order for a plate to react that way you would think it would need massive pressure around the edges. To be in someone's hands and break that way in equally small pieces is very odd indeed.

Dangers of approaching all this with religion

To use religion in the exploration and explanation of paranormal happenings is both dangerous and fruitless. Religion is a unique invention of *humans* so it is in no way a part of the paranormal equation. The history of the subject demonstrates that when religion is commandeered to handle hauntings and other supernatural events, it falsely appears to work and then, only for a very specific reason that has nothing to do with divine intervention. Religion's impact on the people themselves is what then helps counteract the entity—but temporarily. Because the people—those who were haunted—didn't change, the phenomena will soon return. One needs to address the actual issue—the entity or force and its incursion into someone's life and territory. Religion masks that because by its nature it focuses on "fighting the paranormal with the paranormal"—the power of the god figure. Successful understanding of the phenomena must focus on the phenomena. Interestingly, the religious approach relinquishes any responsibility for understanding anything about it on the part of humans. That reflects, perhaps, the basic weakness of religion, in general.

[Shane has a 100-percent success rate and never uses religion because it is not necessary. Entities are not Bible readers. Entities do not share human religious values. Our human belief systems cannot be imposed on them and never are.]

Chapter 16

The Investigation

"There is something we are missing. There is
something special about this land."
—Shane Sirois

In 2005, after Donna read one of Paul Eno's books, she contacted him
and Ben Eno about the various goings-on at her house. The men visited
the family home and definitely felt the presence of some very active areas
of the house. Ben, being much younger then, wouldn't talk much during investigations unless he and Paul debriefed later. So, after they left,
he reported seeing a figure rushing across the bathroom entrance in the
home. And as you know by now, that was only the beginning.

The Three-Point Flap

Paul Eno offered the following opinion:

*This is the "core" in our opinion. From what we can see, the ac-
tual intersect area spills out over a much wider area. So far, we have
never really been able to pin down the "boundaries" of the flap area.
How do you tell if the apparitions in Jane Doe's house in Torrington
are manifesting through the same intersect system as the Bigfoot in
some field in Goshen or Litchfield? So this is a flap "center" and flaps
can overlap. In the end, as I say in lectures, this is the normal state
of the world: the whole thing is "haunted." That's more complicated
by the apparent fact that some people are "magnets" for
intersects. That's why they're "psychic" or "haunted" themselves.*

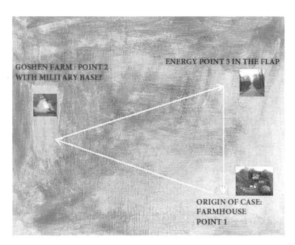

Figure 16-1. *An illustration of where the three-point flap appears to be. Of course, this represents heightened activity since we know the paranormal is everywhere and points don't dictate its whereabouts. Illustration used by permission of Cynthia Smith.*

Shane Sirois, an accomplished paranormal investigator joined the investigation team. I was excited at that prospect since I lectured with Shane and was captivated by his insights into the workings of these parallel world intersects. Shane was excited too since this would be a rare opportunity to gather evidence and study, rather than merely help a family, providing no focus on evidence or further insight or exploration. After all, parasite cases are pretty textbook for Shane; he cleaned up the mess of many well-known paranormal giants seen on TV and is followed with zeal by admirers everywhere. Little do people know how far off these TV giants are in their approach and their understanding of basic parasite infestations and other paranormal occurrences. Of course, those are the very reasons they often fail.

Shane showed me a map and got excited as he pointed and said, "So my long-held theory is that over 90 percent of my most active cases of paranormal activity had water nearby, particularly a river or stream that had a direction of flow that pointed toward the property and curved away." This house has not one, not two, but three such geo-physical characteristics! They do not need to be raging rivers. They just need to be pointed directly towards or directly away from the area under consideration. In cases of waterfalls, neighborhoods are most often haunted. In the case of this farmhouse, my best guess is, due to the severity of the supporting elements, that is also the situation. There is an abundance of water in the area. There are springs directly across the street from the farmhouse, a river behind that, a brook behind the house, a lake above them, and below them the river conjunction that flows into the West Branch of the Naugatuck River.

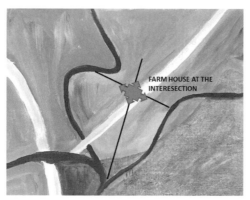

Figure 16-2. *This is an illustration of the mapped area near the farmhouse with the water placement and flow that Shane is referring to. Illustration used by permission of Cynthia Smith.*

Findings, Evidence, and Insight

Before Shane entered the house for the first time, he felt the presence of a train outside; of course, there was none. He entered into the kitchen, which had once been a general store. He related his feeling about a train. He had no idea that Donna had heard and seen that same phantom train go by several times.

We do know that the environment in the house attracts what enters into the home when the "door" is open. Dysfunction brings the more negative entities inside. Donna and Bob were the perfect couple to be there and their family is the main reason why most of the phenomena experienced there is more fascinating in nature than malevolent.

In the basement, Shane saw someone who was a few inches shorter than him pass him inside the door. He also instinctively knew and felt there was a missing piece or something significant about the land. In surveying the inside of the home and taking the tour, he felt it the strongest in two places: the den and the tool area in the basement. The investigation team set up the equipment there and returned to the kitchen to talk, allowing time to pass, hoping to perhaps catch something or someone in the act. When we went back downstairs to check the equipment a short while later, we found the door to a metal cabinet just inside the entry door to the tool room had opened—blocking our entrance to the room. We established that no one had been down there since we were last there. I tested the cabinet and the door and it determined that it was not a loose or freely swinging door. It was sitting perfectly level and shut firmly. I could not reproduce the movement of the door using gravity even assuming the door might have been open a bit to begin with.

Shane sensed that there was somebody relaxing in the den just watching us. Paul and Ben had sensed that also, and Donna commented that it is one of the most active rooms in the house.

Figure 16-3. *The cabinet at the entrance to the workshop in its closed position.*

Later, when we went back to check the equipment in the basement, we found that the brand new batteries we had inserted into the audio recorder were fried. Because of that, nothing had been recorded. We replaced them with new batteries and hoped that they would work that time. It was the unit we placed in the basement area where Shane felt the most activity.

During an overnight visit, Shane stayed up most of the night. At one point he heard a little girl say, "I just want to go out and play." It had been loud enough to be heard through the closed dining room door.

Paul recalled that he had heard about this little girl before, but

Figure 16-4. *The cabinet at the entrance to the workshop as we found it. No one was in the basement until we went back down to check on the equipment.*

Figure 16-5. *A view of the workshop.*

never encountered her. "I don't trust little girls in these situations," he said. "As you know, they might not be little girls. They could be scary."

Of course I had to joke that the same can be said of bigger girls.

All kinds of people and beings pass through that house routinely. With the exception of deceased members of Donna's family, Paul thinks a few are old general-store customers. "I've encountered mostly non-humans, either benign or indifferent, and they usually aren't English-speakers."

Figure 16-6. *The kitchen; a long forgotten general store.*

Shane's Comments on the First Visit

When I first got there and was given the tour I felt nothing right away, which is not unusual. Bill had asked me to see if I felt anything in a particular spot in the basement where he, Paul, and Ben all had an experience. I did not feel anything unusual there during that visit. I did, however, feel something pretty strong just on the other side of the wall in the workshop. I felt it strongest right in front of that adjoining wall. That was within twenty minutes of my arrival. I went upstairs to get some equipment to take down there. When we returned, a metal door to a locker/cabinet had been opened up, blocking the entrance to the workshop room. That door does not move easily and did NOT open on its own. It was the same room in which I had the feeling earlier.

Donna stated during my visit that she and her daughter would both get freaked out in the little area that separates the two larger areas of the basement. It did not surprise me because I could feel elevated levels of

Figure 16-7. *The basement door where the image appeared by the motion activated camera we had set up.*

Figure 16-8. *The basement door with the image caught by the motion activated camera. Look at the top row, third window to the right.*

EMF in that area. When she said that, I asked Bill to remind me to bring my EMF detector down there so I could show him something about that area. As has been established, elevated and fluctuating levels of EMF can stimulate paranoia. I could feel it and I did not associate it with a "presence" of any kind. This was its own radiating energy not associated with anything else, but could certainly contribute to the mechanics of this home's phenomena. My detector proved what I suspected. We had pretty substantial highs and lows that were continuous and were not coming from wiring or other equipment. Before leaving that area I saw a male figure move in front of the basement door from left to right. The figure was approximately five feet, eight inches tall and had dark hair. I did not catch much more detail than that as it was brief. I set up the motion-activated camera in that direction and captured the image in the basement window. That image is what triggered the camera to take three consecutive photos. Also, both in the basement and outside I feel the sense of urgency. It is as if people are hiding or running from something. It almost feels like they are fleeing toward the rear of the property.

The den to the far right of the house has a strong, almost constant presence. I felt a number of different things from time to time in the area of the dining room and den, but whatever/whoever is in the den seems to have been and is a constant fixture. It feels very much like they are just overlooking everything; like they are dedicated it.

Outside I felt there was so much going on around me it became frustrating because I felt I should be seeing so much more than I was able to. It was as if there was so much we were not seeing, yet it was there and very real. It remained very busy out there. There was also something out there that felt afraid. Something was scared and desperate.

Once everyone went to bed I eventually laid down on the cot so I would not disturb anyone. I stayed awake most of the night. After laying there for quite some time I heard a loud *pop* or *snap*. We are all very familiar with this and it can either come at the beginning of an activity or at the end of it. Right after that pop something was dropped at my feet. It sounded like a coin or a ring. It bounced several times and finally came to rest. I was shocked it did not wake anyone. (Evidently this author does quite well in a haunted house. I fell right to sleep and never woke up.) I searched for it at the time and again in the morning and found nothing. The noise had been loud and distinct. A little while later I heard the girl's voice. "I just want(ed) to go out and play." I heard her at a very good volume, just on the other side of the dining room/living room door. About 10 to 15 minutes after that I heard what sounded just like a large turkey roaster tin being thrown to the floor and then kicked. Once again I was shocked that nobody even stirred in the house. It was loud and was coming from the kitchen. In the morning I inspected the kitchen and I was not surprised to see two tins sitting on top of the cabinets. They both were dented. I am not suggesting the noise I

Figure 16-9. *The den, a very active room in the house.*

heard caused that dent, but it is worth noting as an observation. Coming from the area of the dining room/den, I heard, on two occasions, what sounded like a marble or pebble bouncing on the floor as if it fell or was thrown. I had a few brief run-ins with something that did not feel human. It was all too brief to sense anything more than that.

It's been theorized that because ghosts require the use of energy to appear, and because the impurities in water conduct electricity, ghosts may appear by using that conductivity.

The image we caught in the basement looks like the little girl with long hair and bangs. The other image outside is very bizarre because it is in front of the truck. It is not in the road and the straight edge at its base is not because of the wall or road line like Marc suggested. If you notice, the line also follows the same contour of the hood of my truck. I believe

Figure 16-10. *The motion activated camera is set up to take three photos in a row. This is the first before capturing the phenomena.*

Figure 16-11. *This is the second photo capture in the sequence.*

FIGURE 16-12. *The white figure that passed from left to right. The camera was on the hood of Shane's truck. We ruled out passing cars and other potential causes leaving this photo as a good capture of something paranormal.*

that the infrared signal reflected or was blocked at the base of this figure/ object by the hood of my truck. If you notice it is pitch black between my truck and the lighter part of this capture. In the photos previous to this one, you can clearly see the white snow. This means that either the infrared signal was reflected, blocked, or this thing was casting its own shadow.

Shane's Comments From the Second Visit

It's like they are acknowledging that I am here and go into a corner and hide. We began talking about the workshop and questioned Bob about his experiences there. Bob agreed that the cabinet is very hard to open. He also went on to say that when he worked down there, he sometimes would turn around and the tool he was just using would be gone, only to be found later.

Figure 16-13. *A view of an expansive hallway in the farmhouse. Photo by Ray Szwec.*

We gathered a lot of EVPs (Electronic Voice Phenomenon) in the home. Now that I have been there more than once, I felt even more.

When in an area of the property I could "see" in my head a group of people running away. I have also seen people coming from and moving toward the home. I have seen people of different races and clothing from conflicting time periods and initially was confused by that because the first time had I assumed it was a family. I felt and could see in my head people coming from that same area. I also felt the presence of Native people, particularly Shaman energy. I believe they used this land for its natural properties, which is an open door. [Shane is referring to the portal or door as natural properties.]

I feel a strong protective entity guarding this land as well, which means this wonderful family has been accepted. This place definitely has a bunch of things passing through it. It is very, very active. That is why I think the Natives used this location for ceremony, which in turn makes the phenomena stronger. I *strongly* believe the rivers play a big part in all this activity, but I feel there is something in the ground both at the back toward the right and also in the front. The front yard feels like burial. The back feels like a *giant* doorway.

[When Marc Dantonio first visited there and walked the land, he discovered a hollow section of land in the back. The fascinating part to this is it was located exactly where Shane felt was a critical part to the land—the land in the back on the right!]

Shane on the Use of the "Portal" by Native Americans and Others

That protective energy I feel there is not there to protect the family. It is there protecting the land. Probably put in place by the Native people. The fact that it is not acting aggressively toward the family means they have been accepted.

Many religions invoke protective spirits to guard sacred land or properties. It is very real. Human "spirits" will also

Figure 16-14. *Shane Sirois during the investigation.*

guard land, but I believe in the case of the land the farmhouse is on, there was definitely an invocation because it is not human. It is big and can be nasty if it needs to be.

Here is a story that may illustrate my point: One day, many years ago, I was doing a remodeling job on the exterior of a home. The couple was very well off. The man was a prominent engineer for missile defense and the woman was an extremely intelligent and classy individual. While working outside, I felt the presence of a gigantic entity. It felt protective of the land. I felt this thing so strongly. I

Figure 16-15. *From left to right: Shane Sirois, Bill Hall, and Marc Dantonio during the investigation.*

Figure 16-16. *The cameras all set up to capture evidence. Of course prior to being ready to record, a black figure passed across the upstairs landing while everyone in the house was in the kitchen.*

believe it could have ripped trees out of the ground and thrown them at me if it had wanted to. Obviously I was no threat to it so "it" just let me know it was there. After several days of such experiences, I had to ask the woman in question.

"This might sound totally bizarre to you, but I am a scientific, paranormal researcher and possess a high degree of sensitivity to such things. I feel a very strong presence in your back yard. It is big, powerful, and can be nasty if it needs to be. I know that probably sounds crazy, but it is so real to me that I had to talk with you about it. Does that sound crazy to you?"

She grasped her chin with her thumb and index finger pointing up over her lips. "Now...why would that sound crazy if I was the one that put it there?"

It turned out that she was the Ultra High Priestess of the North Eastern Wiccan Religion. She invoked the protector. The reason it was in the back was to protect her hidden alter out in the woods. I had felt its presence at the spot directly in front of the opening to the path, which lead into the trees.

A Belief Isn't Necessarily a Valid Belief

Beliefs and religions are just tools. It doesn't matter what they are—religion, Ouija board, and so on—all of them are just tools to focus our attention in the direction of the paranormal. If done properly, such a focus may be rewarding. If given the wrong type of attention, it can backfire and attract a parasite. Think about this: Every single real bad possession came upon somebody that came from an obsessively religious family. Coincidence? No. All of them were extremely religious, but dysfunctional in the way they applied religion to their lives and their children's lives.

I have done tests with unsuspecting people as well. I was a manager for an electronics company many years ago. I told the employees in one of the departments that the building was haunted. I told them specific things. They were mostly Latin women and they became quite nervous. Before you know it, we had actual activity happening. It was very active and one of the employees was on the verge of quitting until I told them I could fix it. Their attention and fear of the subject actually attracted something into the space, which was, of course, the purpose of the experiment. So hauntings themselves can be reverse engineered.

Shane on the Audio Evidence

There are some pretty distinct voices recorded in the house and others that are distorted, but there is clearly saying, "Harry…(hid it) or (hit it)…HARRY." The name Harry comes up quite a few times. There is a frustrated parental voice that says, "Get to bed!" Some of the other things you can hear are: "I like her," "I'll keep her," "I'm trapped," and others. One of the most angry ones is "I don't give a f*ck about you." The clearest is of someone whispering messages. There is one that sounds angry. There is one that sounds like hooves clip-clopping around.

Audio obtained from a later visit gave insight into Harry. There was a clear audio saying, "Harry hit her." Not like somebody instructing Harry to hit a girl, but like somebody describing that Harry, in fact, hit a female. I do pick up on a male in that basement whenever I go there. Dark hair, medium build, and about 5 foot, 8 inches tall.

Another of the angrier audios sounds like "Get out of here—it's my house."

On our Friday the 13th overnight, we picked up Harry in the den, where Shane felt the presence of a man and placed the spirit box and speaker in that spot to capture any responses to our questions:

"What is your name?" Shane clearly annunciated.

"Harry" we heard as a response. There was static at all times except when we asked direct questions.

"What is your name?" Shane repeated.

"Harry" was the response again and this time the voice was clearer with a distinctive pitch to it.

"Are you Harry Wilcox? I asked.

"Yes" was the almost immediate response.

[Donna shared earlier with us that there was a Harry that once lived there and may have helped build the farmhouse! His name is Harold Wilcox. In searching the historical records, the land purchase originated with William Wilcox.]

Next, Shane told me he was going to really try to connect. He closed his eyes with his hands on his forehead in concentration, while I remained silent for him. The static from the spirit box that was continuous and predictable suddenly changed right after he started focusing his thoughts. It started pulsing in a rhythmic pattern. It was going crazy with diverse sounds and activity! When Shane finally stopped concentrating, the static returned to its previous predictable steadiness. As a magician, if I didn't know Shane and had not worked with him previously, I wouldn't have believed it. I understand if you do not believe it, but it is true and very real.

~

This investigation could go on for countless generations. And besides, the family members are now our friends. Be sure to subscribe to my newsletter at *williamjhallauthor.com* to keep up with this exciting active case.

Chapter 17

I Don't Know What Universe You're Living In

"When we hear the word 'universe,' we think that means everything: every star, every galaxy, everything that exists. But in physics, we've come upon the possibility that what we've long thought to be everything may actually only be a small part of something that is much, much bigger."
—Brian Greene

Do I, Marc Dantonio, believe there are spirits? Not necessarily. That's my answer and now I will try to explain why. I have had relevant experiences right here in my current house. I have seen and heard things that had no "rationally explainable" reason to be seen or heard. There is a back story to this that I need to share with you before I proceed. In simple terms, some years ago I had something go wrong with my brain. There was a growth in my brain from birth and it moved into the wrong spot. It is called a colloid cyst, which is a fluid-filled sac in the brain which, from time to time, can vary in size (more fluid, less fluid). When in the "wrong" spot, or of the wrong size, it can produce pressure, which, in turn, can cause brain function problems. As I suggested, mine migrated to a very, very bad spot. The doctor predicted I had less than eight weeks to live unless it was removed immediately. I was to go back the following day and he would go through the entire procedure with me—a very delicate and time-consuming operation as it turned out. I had the surgery. It was pronounced successful. Hmmm?

Even as a child, I have never been afraid of, or even worried much about what comes after life. I have always felt like I am manipulating a puppet from within this body. I never felt like this body was *me*. The "me" was some entity that controlled the body—like a master puppeteer. When, after the surgery, I started to have strange experiences; I characterized them as stemming from my body and not from "me." They *were* happening, but they were somehow detached. Let me explain further.

At first I started to hear voices. I wasn't hearing anything directed toward me—no commands, no demands, no reactions to things I said. It was more like I was overhearing other people's conversations. Regardless of their detached nature, they were getting in my way. They were a distraction for me. I was having trouble focusing and the quality of my work was suffering. I went through a period of two or three months when I couldn't really concentrate at all. I had to constantly listen to music to drown out the voices. They would distract me to the point where I would be in my office working on something and I would hear people all the way upstairs talking among themselves. Over time they became louder and louder. At home at night I would catch myself thinking, "Why are the kids still up? It's 11:30 at night." So, I would go upstairs and it would be dark. Everything was turned off. The kids were asleep.

It is important to understand that the voices are not in my head. They originate in the space about me. I can pinpoint the direction of their source with my ears.

About a year ago, I started to catch fleeting images of little things out of the corners of my eyes. At first I wrote it off to being tired. I talked to the eye doctor, but my symptoms were all wrong. I didn't see the expected lights or little flashes or distorted lines. I saw flashes of people and animals—vague, though discernable images. There would appear to be someone walking by, but upon close inspection no one would be there. So, naturally, I thought I was just fatigued. Everyone sees things outside their vision when they are exhausted. Then I started seeing things in my direct vision—straight ahead of me. And they were persistent. I would move my head to the left and to the right and the images persisted in three dimensions.

One morning, I was brushing my teeth in the bathroom and I turned around. There was a woman standing there—a total stranger, dressed oddly. It scared the heck out of me. I looked at her. I couldn't see flesh—it wasn't that. It was semi-transparent. The movie *The Abyss* presents the closest example I can give. It resembled the "face" on the water creature. Imagine that without the sheen. That's what these look like. There is no refraction through them. I can't discern the three-dimensional quality that well because it's all bound up in the translucency. Even so, based on the cut of the image—the shoulders and the general form—it looked like a women. She wasn't looking *at* me. It appeared that she was looking *through* me at something else—experiencing some other image, as if I were not there, that my substance was fully inconsequential.

More than fascinating me or startling me, that experience frightened me. Certainly something fully unexplainable was going on and the unexplainable was never comfortable—good.

So, I consulted a neurologist and told him that I had begun seeing and hearing things. I went into great detail. My experiences puzzled the doctor who had removed the cyst. He said the part of the brain effected by that operation might impact my memory somewhat, but not other brain functions. He ordered an MRI but was unable to find anything out of the ordinary. A follow-up CAT scan was also clear.

Although I had tried sincerely to search for a definitive answer, I was unable to find a doctor who was willing to offer as much as a "likely" opinion. In fact, none of them had a clue and most admitted to that.

Because the medical profession had no answers for me I would look elsewhere. The next step in my search came about in the following way.

I was in my workshop working on a prop for a movie, having a ball. It was 3 o'clock in the afternoon and I was in high gear. All of a sudden I saw a dog-like something walk into the room. It remained low to the floor and expressed no apparent interest in me or in the specifics of the surroundings. It was semitransparent, looking to be a Pekinese by the way it moved and its general ball-like shape. It completed a tight a circle—the way dogs will do—and then laid down. I stopped working and studied it, leaning my head to the left and to the right. Whatever it was clearly existed in three-dimensional space.

My first reaction was to reference some personally present medical condition. Perhaps my brain was playing back voices or people or images like latent images. I had heard that sometimes happens as a result of trauma to the brain after surgery. It was, however, sixteen years after the surgery. It came to me that if I was seeing only mental images, I shouldn't be seeing them in three dimensions. It should be like two dimensional snapshots, because my brain can only play back what it had seen. It couldn't play back the *other* side of the dog, which had not been in view, for example. When I moved around it, I *could* see the other side. I walked closer to the dog to check and make sure my observation had been correct. It was. Three dimensions! I rubbed my eyes trying to make certain it was a persistent rather than a transient vision. It was the most persistent of those sorts of experiences that I had ever encountered.

Although I can't explain how the idea came to me, it turned out to be a stroke of genius. I stepped into the dog's space with one foot. I can only explain the experience that followed in this way: When you try to push two north poles from two magnets together it not only takes great force, but typically together they will slide past each other instead of confronting each other head to head—pole surface to pole surface. Molecularly, they are constructed to resist touching each other. That repulsive force you feel is an invariable characteristic of magnets—an unyielding phenomenon of nature.

I felt that same tremendous repulsive force in the back of my heel when I stepped forward to where this thing was. It was some kind of pressure trying to push my foot further forward. It occurred at the exact moment the "dog" stood up and moved away—apparently reacting to me stepping on it or into it or whatever had taken place. My leg became limp and flew out from under me and I fell. When I fell, I grabbed onto the table trying to prop myself up. In the process I wrenched my back.

That condition persisted for months, but hurt back and all, I was absolutely elated. I had just interacted with something totally amazing. I can't make any judgment as to what it was. I do know one thing. It communicated. Rudimentary, but it was communication. I stepped on it—or at least too close to it for its comfort—and it reacted. I looked up in time to see just the last part of it fade away as it ran—vanishing in the center of the room.

I called several astrophysicist colleagues and asked about the current thinking regarding parallel universe theories. The big bang theory is still a theory only because it can't be proved beyond doubt, even though there is a preponderance of evidence, which suggests there was a massive primordial super atom explosion. That state of the multi-universe theory got mixed reviews. One of them—a minority skeptic, if clearly a learned member of his field—said, "I don't know if I buy into that crap. There's no indisputable evidence to support it." So I left it at that for the time being.

Just under a year later, there was a related article in *Science*. The article reported that scientists, in general, do believe in the big bang, *and* further that it most likely spawned multiple universes, not just one. Are those universes spread out side by side? Do they all occupy the same "space" but in different qualities of essence? Could it be possible that some "seepage" between them can occur?

Epilogue

When it comes right down to it, this is no story—it is a glimpse at life and, therefore, it never really ends. The book may stop, but this very special area of land and its phenomena remains. The nature of the activities discernible in the paranormal flap may vary from time to time and even come and go, but that is also a continuance of a kind—eternal, perhaps.

It is difficult to summarize that which we fully understand. The subject we have pursued here is far less understood them most and is therefore far more difficult to summarize in any sort of conclusive manner. Perhaps the great legacy of this material is not the answers discovered, but the indisputable questions it continues to raise and the openness of inquiry it continues to require.

Meeting and spending time with the Fillies has been a fulfilling and enriching experience for me. To spend time at a paranormal crossroad has been life altering for me. The family says—and sincerely so, I believe—that they consider me part of their family now (you see, wonders never cease!).

Throughout this investigation into the paranormal I have been privileged to meet and grow close to many fine people. In addition to the extended Fillie family, I have also grown closer to Paul, Ben, Shane, and Marc. Working together and pondering shared experiences has formed a useful, educational, fulfilling, and irrevocable bond.

This experience became my own Lindley Street. It was my firsthand junket into the realms of often indistinguishable—though clearly present—entities. It was generally a kind and comfortable encounter for me and I would like to think it was for "them" as well. I hope my depiction of them as *entities* presents a proper characterization that leads us away from "ghosts stalking the night" to a broader, more diverse portrait of what may lay beyond most human senses.

Having the privilege to spend hours with Shane Sirois has been an apprenticeship like no other. Shane is so far advanced in his comprehension of what is really going on that he often exposes the typical ghost hunters as stumbling amateurs.

Likewise, it has been a pleasure to work with Marc Dantonio, who has experienced so much of the paranormal and still remains comfortably skeptical and objective. His generosity of time, in the use of his drones and pointed conversations, has been both entertaining and insightful.

I am proud to call them both friends.

My hope is that this work provides the reader and student alike a rare insight into the reality of living, for five decades, at the epicenter of a paranormal flap. I make no pretense of having produced a horror story worthy of a Stephen King novel. My intention has been to present the unembellished truth as I have been able to discover, pursue, and verify it.

Even sans the horrifying demons and heart-stopping scenes from a Hollywood production, I hope it has provided a wonderful and fulfilling journey for those of you who have accompanied me through these pages and prefer a true investigation over an Amityville Horror–type production.

Before *The Haunted House Diaries*, I laughed, loved, and wondered in a way that I believed was imaginative and delightful—pragmatic, even. After this experience, however, I laugh deeper and love in a new and more profound way. My imagination is now freed beyond anything I had conceived of before. It is fueled by this new reality that calls out to be probed, and if not fully understood, to be appreciate more fully, and described more completely with new and more relevant theories derived from our carefully guided experiences with the paranormal—the new, less frightening, and even more fascinating paranormal. Don't be scared. After all, nothing in the paranormal can manifest pain as debilitating and devastating as lost love.

Appendix I

Initial Family Interview

CASE# 200518
(transcription)
Name: Robert and Donna Fillie
Address:
E-mail:
Phone:
*

Preface: Contacted by Donna Fillie in June 2005 after she read *Foot-steps*. She believes multiverse is only explanation for various phenomena in house and on property.

Initial Check: August 27, 2005
Ben and I arrived just past 11 am. Toured house with Donna. Hotspots in kitchen and in daughter's living room. Also upstairs on landing, in front bedroom (child's), and rear bedroom. Both bedrooms face south. Also at south end of basement.

Initial Interview: August 27, 2005

A. THE HOUSE:
1. How long have you lived in the house?
Six generations. Donna for over 60 years.

2. How old is the house?
1793.

3. What do you know about the history of the house or the land?
Started as general store. Donna's ancestors (Randalls) were second owners.
Land used for farming.

4. Are you the first occupants?
No. See above.

5. As far as you know, did any previous occupants report trouble?
Strange events with no apparent pattern as far back as anyone can remember.
Little or nothing overtly negative.

6. As far are you know, are neighbors reporting trouble at their homes?
Will research.

B. THE PEOPLE
1. How many people live in the house?
Five.

2. Please describe them.
Donna, elderly mother, Bob, daughter Michelle, grandson Dale (toddler)
(Donna and Bob married, employed. Michelle divorced. Dale 2+ and still in diapers.)

3. Has any occupant been treated for an unusual medical condition since you have lived in the house?
No.

4. Has any occupant been treated for stress, depression, or any other psychological condition at any time?
No.

5. Are the children, if any, having problems at school?
N/A

6. Do you consider yourselves religious?
Believers but not active in a religious group.

7. Do you belong to a church, temple, mosque, etc.? If so, which one?
Donna tried Ouija board many years before. Interested in paranormal because of experiences in the house. No active involvement.

8. What is your ancestry?
Italian, Irish, English

9. As far as you know, were any of your immediate family or ancestors involved in the occult?
Not particularly.

10. Do you believe in ghosts or evil spirits?
Yes.

11. Do you believe in angels or guardian spirits?
Yes.

12. Do you believe in UFOs?
Yes.

13. Have you ever had a paranormal experience before this? If so, please describe.
As above.

14. Has your electric bill been unusually high lately?
Yes, but depends on time of year and severity of phenomena.

15. Who in the house has had experiences?
All, though Bob tends to ignore.

16. Have any of your neighbors complained of such experiences? Will check if and when possible.

17. How do you feel about your current experience? Afraid, excited, annoyed...?
Not afraid. Used to odd happenings but would like to know the cause, and would like some peace and quiet.

C. THE AREA
1. Are you aware of any reports of any paranormal activity in the area, either past or present (including UFOs, cryptids and/or legends)?
Not at this point.
*

PRIVATE NOTES
House definitely active.

1) HOTSPOTS: Ben and I both had typical reactions to intersect areas in Michelle's living room, upstairs rear bedroom, and south basement. Also in north end and lower areas of yard.

2) Struck by positive nature of family, held together by Bob and Donna. Also struck by Dale still in diapers. He was understandably reluctant to talk with strangers, but relates stories of strange figures in his bedroom. Did not seem afraid.

3) Phenomena include sounds of other people, music, odd figures (human and non-human) seen throughout house and outside. Legs hanging from main living room ceiling and seeming to walk. Boxy figures with legs outside windows and near doors. Orbs by the hundreds, in photos and with naked eye. Also moving objects and footsteps in no apparent pattern. Also, Donna has EVPS with what could be human and non-human voices, and videos with lots of orbs.

4) Donna gave us a copy of a record she has kept.

5) Our photos and videos need to be reviewed. But one taken in basement appears to show a tall, robed figure walking across an open space. Will check against still.

6) Recommend continuing with night visits, overnight stays, research into area, etc. Research seismic, hydrology, and soils. History of phenomena in area.

Appendix II

Historical House Records

The date of construction was passed down through the generations as 1793. The historical records reflect the larger side of the house, which includes the bedrooms, kitchen, living room, and downstairs bathroom. This Victorian portion of the house was built in the early 1880s.

The original house, consisting of the den, dining room, and upstairs bedroom and bath was built in 1793.

The city was not interested in that side of the house when they came for the report. The portion of the house built in 1793 was originally the general store, but the city has no records of the outlying areas, homes, or businesses. The historical society records state that the 1880 home replaced an earlier building.

Donna herself took them through the home when they came to compile the historical report.

HISTORIC RESOURCES INVENTORY
BUILDINGS AND STRUCTURES
HIST-6   REV. 6/83

STATE OF CONNECTICUT
CONNECTICUT HISTORICAL COMMISSION
59 SOUTH PROSPECT STREET, HARTFORD, CONNECTICUT 06106
(203) 566-3005

FOR OFFICE USE ONLY	
Town No.:	Site No.:
UTM	
QUAD.	
DISTRICT	IF NR, SPECIFY

DISTRICT □ S □ NR   IF NR, SPECIFY □ Actual   □ Potential

IDENTIFICATION

1. BUILDING NAME (Common)
(Historic) William Wilcox House

2. TOWN / CITY ▇▇▇▇   VILLAGE "West Side"   COUNTY Litchfield

3. STREET AND NUMBER (and / or location) ▇▇▇▇

4. OWNER(S)
Robert and Donna Fillie   □ Public   ☒ Private

5. USE (Present)
Residence   (Historic) Residence

6. ACCESSIBILITY TO PUBLIC: ☒ Yes □ No   EXTERIOR VISIBLE FROM PUBLIC ROAD   INTERIOR ACCESSIBLE □ Yes ☒ No   IF YES. EXPLAIN

7. STYLE OF BUILDING
Vernacular Homestead   DATE OF CONSTRUCTION c. 1880

8. MATERIAL(S) (Indicate use or location when appropriate)

☒ Clapboard	□ Asbestos siding	□ Brick	□ Other (Specify)
□ Wood shingle	□ Asphalt siding	□ Fieldstone	
□ Board & batten	□ Stucco	□ Cobblestone	
☒ Aluminum siding	□ Concrete Type:	☒ Cut stone Type: Random ashlar	

9. STRUCTURAL SYSTEM

□ Wood frame	□ Post and beam	☒ Balloon
□ Load-bearing masonry	□ Structural iron or steel	
□ Other (Specify)		

DESCRIPTION

10. ROOF (Type)

☒ Gable	□ Flat	□ Mansard	□ Monitor	□ Sawtooth
□ Gambrel	□ Shed	□ Hip	□ Round	□ Other (Specify)

(Material)

□ Wood shingle	□ Roll asphalt	□ Tin	□ Slate
☒ Asphalt shingle	□ Built up	□ Tile	□ Other (Specify)

11. NUMBER OF STORIES 2   APPROXIMATE DIMENSIONS 46' x 30'

12. CONDITION (Structural)   (Exterior)
□ Excellent ☒ Good □ Fair □ Deteriorated   □ Excellent ☒ Good □ Fair □ Deteriorated

13. INTEGRITY (Location) ☒ On original site □ Moved   WHEN?   ALTERATIONS ☒ Yes □ No   IF YES, EXPLAIN Shed at right/rear incorporated into house

14. RELATED OUTBUILDINGS OR LANDSCAPE FEATURES

□ Barn	☒ Shed	□ Garage	□ Other landscape features or buildings (Specify)
□ Carriage house	□ Shop	□ Garden	

15. SURROUNDING ENVIRONMENT

☒ Open land	□ Woodland	☒ Residential	☒ Scattered buildings visible from site
□ Commercial	□ Industrial	□ Rural	□ High building density

16. INTERRELATIONSHIP OF BUILDING AND SURROUNDINGS This structure is situated near a bend in the road in a rural residential area not far from the hamlet of Drakeville.

(OVER)

17. OTHER NOTABLE FEATURES OF BUILDING OR SITE (interior and/or exterior)

██████████████████████████ is a large two-story vernacular homestead residence with a gable roof, oriented gable end to the street. The structure rests on a random ashlar granite foundation and is sheathed with wooden clapboards. The building incorporates a single-story, full-width, shallow hip roof porch with square columns and turned ballusters. Window sash is of 2/2 configuration. Architectural and decorative features include a one-and-one-half-story gable roof ell at the right, plain flat window casings and corner boards, 6/6 sash in the ell peak, and an entry door containing small colored border lights in the upper glass panel. Documentary evidence suggests that a portion of this house may date from an earlier period.

18. ARCHITECT   BUILDER

19. HISTORICAL OR ARCHITECTURAL IMPORTANCE

Between 1877 and the 1890s William Wilcox acquired several parcels of land from older Torrington families such as the Fylers, Barbers, Reeds, and Gillettes. The family had arrived in Torrington only recently. William likely erected this house c. 1880, replacing an earlier dwelling on the property he had purchased.

The structure is architecturally significant as a fine example of the vernacular homestead farmhouses constructed in rural Torrington in the latter decades of the nineteenth century. The building is historically important in documenting the selling off of land held for generations by early Torrington families, a process which accelerate after the Civil War, as well as the declining status of farming in the same period. By this period farmers had become quite conservative in their architectural tastes and eschewed the more up-to-date styles favored by urban residents.

SOURCES

Orcutt, History of Torrington
Torrington Town Meeting Records
Torrington Land Records
Torrington Assessor's Records
City Maps: 1815 (manuscript), 1852 (Clark), 1874 (Beers)

PHOTO

PHOTOGRAPHER   DATE
Geoffrey Rossano   March 1994
VIEW   NEGATIVE ON FILE
East   1-36A

COMPILED BY

NAME   DATE
Geoffrey Rossano/Joan Baldwin   February 1994
ORGANIZATION
Torrington Historic Preservation Trust
ADDRESS
P.O. Box 1233, Torrington, Conn. 06790

20. SUBSEQUENT FIELD EVALUATIONS

21. THREATS TO BUILDING OR SITE

[X] None known   [ ] Highways   [ ] Vandalism   [ ] Developers   [ ] Other_____
[ ] Renewal   [ ] Private   [ ] Deterioration [ ] Zoning   Explanation_____

HST 6 REV. 6/83 (Back)

Appendix III

Bonus Features

Audio and Video Evidence

This book includes special features for you. You can access the actual video evidence, as well as EVP audio evidence. Findings will be added on this special web page as the investigation is ongoing (since I am now part of the family!). These bonus features are available for you at *www.williamjhallauthor.com/bonus.html*

Want More Haunted Diary Insight?

Be sure to visit *www.williamjhallauthor.com* to see where William will be appearing.

Speaking Events

William J. Hall is available for speaking events on this fascinating paranormal flap as well as on the Bridgeport Poltergeist (Lindley Street) case. Contact Bill at bill@worldsmosthauntedhouse.com for more information.

Bulk Sales for Your Group

If you are interested in bulk sales for your group, book club, paranormal society, magazine, or fundraiser, please contact New Page Books at (800) 227–3371.

If You Enjoyed This Book...

Please review it online at Amazon.com or BarnesandNoble.com. Thank you!

Be sure to read William Hall's *The World's Most Haunted House: The True Story of the Bridgeport Poltergeist on Lindley Street*. It's available wherever books are sold.

Appendix IV

Litchfield Hills Phenomena Reporting Procedure

If you have or know someone who lives in the area of the paranormal flap (or did at one time), please contact Bill using the contact form located at *www.williamjhallauthor.com* so we can add to this investigation.

Bibliography

The primary data source for the diary sections are letters kept and assembled by Donna Fillie over a period of decades.

Additional sources include interviews with the following people:

- Paul F. Eno
- Benjamin Eno
- Bob Fillie
- Michelle L. Carpenter
- Diane Randall
- Marc Dantonio
- Shane Sirois
- Greg Harold
- Phantom roadblock male witness (wished to remain anonymous)
- Phantom roadblock female witness (wished to remain anonymous)
- Neighbors (wished to remain anonymous)

Additional titles include:

Eno, Paul F. *Faces at the Window*. Moorhead, Minn.: New River Press, 1998.

———. *Footsteps in the Attic: More First-Hand Accounts of the Paranormal in New England*. Moorhead, Minn.: New River Press, 2002.

———. *Turning Home: God, Ghosts and Human Destiny*. Moorhead, Minn.: New River Press, 2006.

Harold, Gregory. *The Alien Connection*. Indianapolis, Ind.: Dog Ear Publishing, LLC, 2009.

———. *Harold's Mystery* (Video). Indianapolis, Ind.: Dog Ear Publishing, LLC, 2012.

Houdini, Harry. *A Magician Among the Spirits*. New York: Harper and Brothers, 1924.

Kim, Meeri. "MIT Scientists Implant a False Memory Into a Mouse's Brain." *The Washington Post*, July 25, 2013.

Noonan, David. "Meet the Two Scientists Who Implanted a False Memory Into a Mouse." *Smithsonian Magazine*, November 2014.

Sirois, Shane. *Trueghost.com.*

INDEX

ABOUT THE AUTHOR

William J. Hall returns to bring us another profound investigation into the unknown. His previous work, *The World's Most Haunted House: The True Story of the Bridgeport Poltergeist on Lindley Street,* is a paranormal bestseller. Hall is professionally equipped to recognize trickery. After more than 25 years as a performing magician, he knows how to create and recognize illusions. He is experienced in researching the unexplained, from folklore and urban legend, to fortune telling, the pyramids, and other mysterious tales. His syndicated 1990s column, "Magic and the Unknown," ran for six years in multiple newspapers in his home state. Hall has two sons and resides in Plainville, Connecticut.

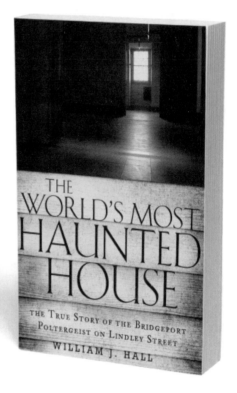

ALSO FROM NEW PAGE BOOKS